# Pages of Promises

Joe and Brenda Henderson

Copyright © 2018 Joe and Brenda Henderson

(Previously published under the title, *Petals of Promises*, this version contains corrections, revisions, and minor changes, creating a book suitable for both men and women, whether in groups, families, or as individuals.)

Author photo: Annika J Photography

Cover design: Kindle Direct Publishing

All rights reserved. No portion of this material may be reproduced or distributed without the written permission of Joe and/or Brenda Strohbehn Henderson and/or his/her/their legal representative(s).
Brief portions may be quoted for review purposes.

Scripture quotations taken from the Amplified® Bible (AMP),
copyright © 2015 by The Lockman Foundation
Used by permission. www.Lockman.org.

Scripture quotations are from the ESV® Bible (The Holy Bible, English Standard Version®), copyright © 2001 by Crossway, a publishing ministry of Good News Publishers. Used by permission. All rights reserved.

Verses and passages quoted from the King James Version (KJV)
are in the public domain.

NASB: Scripture taken from the NEW AMERICAN STANDARD BIBLE®, copyright © 1960, 1962, 1963, 1968, 1971, 1972, 1973, 1975, 1977, 1995 by The Lockman Foundation. Used by permission.

Scripture taken from the New King James Version®. Copyright © 1982 by Thomas Nelson. Used by permission. All rights reserved.

ISBN: 9781790373420

To Kaleb Joshua, Makayla Mae, and Lucy Margaret,
who bring this great-uncle and great-aunt great joy

May you daily find your greatest delight
in Christ and in His Word

---

And with our deepest gratitude for
Gus and Bonnie Jean Henderson
and
Ben and Lorraine Strohbehn

The love our parents had for their spouses
brought them great joy as they served the Lord together

We attribute to their teaching and example
the great joy we found
in writing this book together

# CONTENTS

Introduction ........................................................................................ 3

January 1 ............................................................................................ 9

February 1 ........................................................................................ 40

March 1 ............................................................................................ 68

April 1 .............................................................................................. 99

May 1 ............................................................................................. 129

June 1 ............................................................................................ 160

July 1 ............................................................................................. 190

August 1 ........................................................................................ 221

September 1 ................................................................................... 252

October 1 ....................................................................................... 282

November 1 ................................................................................... 313

December 1 ................................................................................... 343

Scripture Index .............................................................................. 375

About the Authors ......................................................................... 381

"The future is
as bright
as the
promises
of God."

—Adoniram Judson

# INTRODUCTION

Adoniram Judson (1788–1850), missionary to Burma (now Myanmar), is attributed with saying, "The future is as bright as the promises of God." This is not only wise; it is true. Because God's Word is true, we can be certain that He will be true to His Word.

The writing we do on our blog and in our books springs from the faith that we share in Jesus Christ and from the truths we read in God's Word. The promises contained in this book come directly from those Scriptures. We share thoughts, lessons, or personal illustrations with a desire of showing you, the reader, that these promises and truth-promises (promises resulting from truth) do not change, and they are yours (as a child of God) to claim.

However, if you are not yet a person of faith (a believer in Jesus Christ and a follower of Him), these promises will be merely "inspirational" rather than spiritual in their impact.

First Corinthians 5:17 (NASB) states: "Therefore if anyone is in Christ, he is a new creature; the old things passed away; behold, new things have come." In other words, your life is changed, different, new when you are "in Christ."

So what does it mean to be "a new creature"? Matthew Henry, in his *Commentary on the Whole Bible*, writes that it is: "a thorough change of the heart." In this case, the heart no longer lives for sin and its temporal pleasures but for Christ and His eternal treasures.

Because of the sin of Adam, the first man created by God and the first to choose his own selfish desires over the commands of God (see Genesis, chapters 2 and 3), all humans are born with sinful hearts. A holy God, however, cannot look on sin and demands that there be a payment for the sin—death. Try as you might in your own strength, you can never be good enough on your own, do enough right things, or follow enough rules and regulations to earn your way into His favor.

So this amazing, compassionate, loving God sent His Son, Jesus, from heaven (see Luke 2) to come to earth and live among humankind (even though He Himself was one with God). Knowing that you could never merit His favor, God sacrificed His own Son (His holy, sinless Son, Jesus) to be the One to die so that you, and *all* of humankind, could have your sin-debt paid in full and could be forgiven of the sins that, from birth, have been your very nature. Christ died the most horrid of deaths—He was tortured and nailed to a cross—but because He is very God Himself, He did not remain dead but rose from the dead (just like the Bible promised that He would)! Not long after this miraculous resurrection from the grave, He ascended into heaven to be with God, His Father, and to intercede on our behalf. Because of this death, burial, and resurrection, God now offers you a pardon for your sins!

That, friend, is a gift that simply requires your using the faith that He gives you to believe Him and to accept this offer of being saved ("salvation") from the penalty for your sins! It is a gift of pure grace! The Bible, God's Word, states: "For by grace you have been saved through faith; and that not of yourselves, it is the gift of God" (Ephesians 2:8, NASB).

In Acts 16, two followers of Christ were asked how someone might become a follower of Christ, accept this grace-given gift of God, and know this forgiveness of sins. Their reply? "They said, 'Believe in the Lord Jesus, and you will be saved…'" (Acts 16:31).

Have you accepted this gift of forgiveness and eternal life in heaven? If so, we would love to hear your faith story. Feel free to send us a note at: PetalsfromtheBasket@gmail.com.

If you have not yet chosen to turn away from ("forsake") your sins, accept God's free gift of salvation, and follow after Christ Jesus as your Savior (the only One Who has the ability to save you from the punishment of sin), please feel free to e-mail us with any questions you many have (PetalsfromtheBasket@gmail.com).

But you don't have to wait to hear back from us. You can pray right where you are and let God know that you desire to repent of your sins (i.e., choose to turn away from them), that you believe that Christ died to pay for your sins, and that you accept His free gift of salvation. And then, as the men in Acts 16:31 told the man who asked them the way of salvation, "you will be saved!"

"You crown the year
with Your goodness,
and Your paths
drip with abundance."

—Psalm 65:11, NKJV

January 1 – December 31

———————

365 Devotional Thoughts

on the

Promises of God

# JANUARY 1

Titus 1:2, NASB:
"In the hope of eternal life, which God, who cannot lie, promised long ages ago."

———

You're here—on this first day of the year—because you want to learn, grow, and move forward in your walk with God. That makes this verse (Titus 1:2) one of the most important verses of the year. If God were to lie to you, your year would be bleak. If He promised that He would never leave or forsake you (which He promised you in Deuteronomy 31:6) but then left you without His help or His presence, you would have no foundation on which to stand.

But the powerful (and almost easy to pass over) truth of this verse—"who cannot lie"—means that every promise God makes to you is a promise that He will keep.

Every. Promise.

It does not say that He *will not* lie. To do so would imply that even though He *won't*, He *could*.

It emphatically states: "who cannot lie." *Cannot*—does not have the ability to. In other words, His holy character and nature make Him *incapable* of lying.

Oh, friend, what a precious, solid volume of truth into which we may place our pages of promises throughout this year.

He. Cannot. Lie.

Therefore, His promises are true.

—BLH

Today's promise:
God *cannot* lie!

# JANUARY 2

James 1:5, ESV:
"If any of you lacks wisdom, let him ask God, who gives generously to all without reproach, and it will be given him."

---

Have you ever been part of a committee or team trying to come up with a solution for a problem? Have you ever been the one at that meeting with the right answer, but no one knew it, because they wouldn't call on you or stop arguing long enough to hear you out?

In meetings like that you literally want to jump up and shout out, "People! Listen up! Stop talking! I have the answer!"

God must feel the same way—times a gazillion! He confidently, rightfully, lovingly says, "I have the solution, the wisdom, the answer. Just ask."

Yet we sit down here on earth just a-stewin' away about all the what-ifs and if-onlys of life, weighing all the options and seeking advice from every resource available to us.

Well, *almost* every resource. Except the most helpful One.

The One with the answers.

But there He sits, our loving, merciful God, with the very wisdom we are seeking. He not only promises to give that wisdom to us, but he will give it to us "generously" and "without reproach" (meaning that He won't get mad at us for asking or even for asking *again*)!

—BLH

Today's promise:
When you ask for wisdom, God *will* give it to you.

# JANUARY 3

Matthew 6:33, KJV:
"But seek ye first the kingdom of God, and his righteousness; and all these things shall be added unto you."

———

Food, shelter, clothing—"these things" (see Matthew 6:24–33). Yet these are three of the things we frequently fret over or spend more than the appropriate amount of time focusing on.

In this oft-quoted verse, God reminds us to keep our eyes on what matters. When we seek His kingdom above all else and keep our eyes fixed on Jesus, we're less likely to stumble over the comparatively insignificant cares of this world.

He does not promise us that we will be free of problems or that we will be rich. One of my new favorite Bible-study-aid websites is *www.GotQuestions.org*, which is a great resource for personal Bible study questions. When I checked this site for clarification regarding the teaching of this verse, here's what I found: "[This verse] is not a formula for gaining wealth. It is a description of how God works."

This is where our amazing promise-keeping God far exceeds our earthly comprehension of love with His level of care for us. He provides—because He can and because He promises that He will.

—BLH

Today's promise:
Seek God first. He *will* take care of the rest!

# JANUARY 4

Deuteronomy 33:27, KJV:
"The eternal God is thy refuge,
and underneath are the everlasting arms...."

---

Having a loving earthly father, I well remember as a little boy seeking a hiding place behind my father's legs when I was confronted with a scary situation—perhaps a barking dog or a noisy car. I would hold on to those legs and carefully peek around them to see if what had frightened me was gone.

At other times, my father would encourage me to jump into his arms from a high place, declaring, "Don't worry, son; I'll catch ya!"

I don't have my dad here anymore to shield me or to catch me. How wonderful that my eternal Father God is always there when I'm afraid. He is always there to sustain me when I need support or help.

—JGH

Today's promise:
God *is*—and *always will be*—there!

# JANUARY 5

Deuteronomy 31:6, KJV:
"Be strong and of a good courage, fear not, nor be afraid of them: for the Lord thy God, he it is that doth go with thee; he will not fail thee, nor forsake thee."

---

Even though Moses himself would not be entering the Promised Land with the children of Israel, he spoke these words to encourage them before they crossed over into the land that God had promised them. They were spoken by Moses, but they were the promises of God.

Whatever your task, wherever your journey takes you, God will be there. He will go with you.

He is available.

He is able.

Therefore, you don't have to be afraid. When you grow weary, you can find strength and hope in the knowledge of His presence.

But it gets better. Think of the magnitude of that hope. It's as wide, broad, and deep as His immeasurable gifts of grace, strength, mercy, and love.

—BLH/JGH

Today's promise:
God *is* able and available!

# JANUARY 6

Philippians 4:19, ESV:
"And my God will supply every need of yours according to his riches in glory in Christ Jesus."

———

We usually think of this verse when we have a need. We are usually admonished to remember that He supplies our needs, not our wants. And we usually think of this in respect to material needs. All of these reminders are good—and true.

But in this verse, He promises to supply *every* need ("*all* your need," KJV, emphasis mine). Need strength? Need wisdom? Need courage? Need hope? Need love for an enemy?

He will supply it!

—BLH

Today's promise:
God supplies *every* need!

# JANUARY 7

Ephesians 3:20, KJV:
"Now unto him that is able to do exceeding abundantly
above all that we ask or think,
according to the power that worketh in us."

———

At a time in my life when I didn't know *how* to pray—or even feel that I had the strength *to* pray—I saw God fulfill this promise. I was desperate beyond measure to see Him work, but it seemed that I was "prayed out." My thoughts, my requests, and the depth of my desire for an answer just couldn't be put into words.

I had said all that I knew how to say.

But the Holy Spirit, true to His promise (see Romans 8:26), formed my thoughts into words, my desires into passionate requests for which words could not even be uttered, and my longings into the very words that could touch the heart of God.

As only God can do, He did what I would have asked but had no power of my own with which to voice the words. Yet He did above—no, He did "*exceedingly abundantly* above"—not only what I *wanted* to ask but also what I never even *thought* of asking.

Ask. Pour out your heart before Him. He longs to help you.

Just because He can.

—BLH/JGH

Today's promise:
God can do *more* than you can even *ask* Him to do!

# JANUARY 8

Psalm 139:15–18, ESV:
"My frame was not hidden from you, when I was being made in secret, intricately woven in the depths of the earth.
Your eyes saw my unformed substance; in your book were written, every one of them, the days that were formed for me,
when as yet there was none of them. How precious to me are your thoughts, O God! How vast is the sum of them!
If I would count them, they are more than the sand.
I awake, and I am still with you."

---

Today is my birthday. The older I get, the more I realize the gift of each year, month, day—moment. In recent years, I have made it a practice to read Psalm 139 on this day. And each year I stand in greater amazement at the fact that the God of the universe has known me from before my conception.

It's remarkable to me that the psalmist is also overwhelmed by the same facts regarding *his* life. He is clearly awestruck by the fact—as am I—that God thinks about us. His thoughts of us number more than all the grains of sand on all the seashores.

And it doesn't stop there. Each day that we are given life, He is with us. He doesn't walk away from us. He doesn't wean us away from His care as we age. He is still there—year after year, month after month, day after day—moment after moment.

There is great security in the promise that He not only knows me and cares for me; He *thinks* about me!

Now *that's* worth celebrating with gratitude and praise!

—BLH

Today's promise:
God *thinks* about you!

# JANUARY 9

Isaiah 41:13, KJV:
"For I the Lord thy God will hold thy right hand,
saying unto thee, Fear not; I will help thee."

---

The very fact that God promises us His help all but guarantees that we will need it at some point. The amazing element behind this is that God's help is perfectly suited to the season of life and the specific struggle that we are walking through.

In other words, He will help us with major life decisions: whether *to* and/or *where* to attend college, the choice of a mate, our career path, how to train our children, etc.

He will help us when change happens: marriage, divorce, death of a spouse, new career, loss of a job, birth of a child, children leaving home, physical accomplishment, medical problems, and more.

He will help us. Period.

Believe it or not, it gets even better! He doesn't help us from afar. He is right there—close enough to hold our hand. Close enough to listen. Close enough to hear. Walking with us beside the still waters and through the valley of the shadow of death.

Yes, friend, He is there.

—BLH

Today's promise:
God *will* help you—whatever the need!

# JANUARY 10

John 14:3, KJV:
"And if I go and prepare a place for you, I will come again, and receive you unto myself; that where I am, there ye may be also."

---

As a little boy I soon discovered that there was a place my parents would leave me when they took me to church. It was called the nursery. Initially, I didn't like to be dropped off there. There was a lot of crying as parents left their children there and headed off to the "big church" service.

I often joined in on the crying, even though my parents would promise me, "We'll come back and pick you up."

My parents always kept their promise, and I was glad to see them coming down the hallway toward the nursery after the service!

Our Lord Jesus gave a wonderful parent-like promise to His anxious and perplexed disciples just after the Passover supper. He said that He would be going away, but that He would come again. They would one day be reunited with Him.

As His children, we have that same promise!

—JGH

Today's promise:
The Lord *will* return for His children!

# JANUARY 11

Psalm 27:14, NKJV:
"Wait on the Lord; be of good courage,
and He shall strengthen your heart;
wait, I say, on the Lord!"

---

Waiting is probably in my top five least-favorite things—on earth! I want the answer now. I want the test results now. I want to know what will happen tomorrow—now!

But God, in His infinite wisdom and His knowledge of the future, says that He will strengthen my heart as I wait on Him. Because of that, I can courageously stand in this moment, knowing that He is aware of my need, longing, desire.

He is powerful enough to grant strength to my fainting, anxious heart. And He promises to do so.

But He also knows me well enough to know that telling me once is most likely not enough. So He lovingly, patiently, mercifully has the psalmist throw in a second reminder: "Wait, I say, on the Lord!"

My friend, courageously wait with hope.

—BLH

Today's promise:
God *will* strengthen your heart!

# JANUARY 12

Proverbs 16:3, KJV:
"Commit thy works unto the Lord,
and thy thoughts shall be established."

---

It's early enough in the calendar year that some of you may still be working through your goals for the year. Maybe you're valiantly "keeping your resolutions," but perhaps you're like I am, and you're already tweaking your overly idealistic goals to more realistically fit into your not so idealistic days!

Nothing helps me more with setting goals than this verse! This amazing promise from our all-powerful God assures us that if we commit our actions ("works") to Him, He will make certain ("establish") the thoughts and plans that will help us to carry them out.

So set that goal. Be committed to achieving it. And then ask God to fulfill His promise to guide you through the plans (and their ensuing thoughts) that will get you there.

—BLH

Today's promise:
God *will* establish your plans!

# JANUARY 13

Psalm 37:23, KJV:
"The steps of a good man are ordered by the Lord:
and he delighteth in his way."

---

I was being transferred by my airline to the crew base of Boston, Massachusetts. My first priority was to find a good Bible-believing church in which to serve the Lord. My second priority was to look for a place to live near that church.

While traveling to Boston, I was on a layover in Philadelphia and "just so happened" to see a well-known preacher sitting in the passenger waiting area. I introduced myself and told him about my search for a church in the New England area.

He quickly gave me the names of three Christian laymen in the southern region of New Hampshire—all of them were active members of good churches in that area. Through those connections, I found a good church in which to serve and a nice house to call home.

To this day I rejoice in recalling God's direction as He fulfilled the promise that He directs the steps of those who delight in His ways.

—JGH

Today's promise:
God *will* direct your steps!

# JANUARY 14

James 1:25, NASB:
"But one who looks intently at the perfect law, the law of liberty, and abides by it, not having become a forgetful hearer but an effectual doer, this man will be blessed in what he does."

---

When Joe and I were working on this book of daily devotionals, one of our primary goals was to make it practical. However, we would sometimes find ourselves merely writing out "Christianese" or having "getting another one checked off the list" as our motive.

Each time we finished a devotional we would read it to the other person, seeking for input, correction, and even praise. But when the motives or wording were merely enabling us (and thereby those reading what we had written) to know more truth but not encouraging ourselves and others to live it out, we would stop, regroup, and rewrite!

We want God to bless our efforts. We want Him to bless yours. Only when we live out—in our homes, our churches, our communities—what we know to be true will we truly be successful.

—BLH

Today's promise:
God *will* bless the effectual doer of the Word.

# JANUARY 15

Matthew 5:3, AMP:
"Blessed [spiritually prosperous, happy, to be admired] are the poor in spirit [those devoid of spiritual arrogance, those who regard themselves as insignificant], for theirs is the kingdom of heaven [both now and forever]."

---

God says that people who have a humble attitude and a modest opinion of themselves will be happy and will have the kingdom of heaven.

As I go throughout my day, is my self-opinion inflated, exalted, and full of pride? Do I think I'm something that I am not?

People with hearts full of pride and self-exaltation cannot truly be happy, because they are constantly discontent. God's Word declares in 1 Timothy 6:6 (KJV): "But godliness with contentment is great gain."

Ask God today to create in you a clean heart and a right spirit. (See Psalm 51:10.)

—JGH

Today's promise:
God *will* reward a humble heart.

# JANUARY 16

Isaiah 55:11, AMP:
"So will My word be which goes out of My mouth;
It will not return to Me void (useless, without result),
Without accomplishing what I desire,
And without succeeding in the matter for which I sent it."

---

I'm grateful that my parents frequently answered my questions with, "Let's see what the Bible says."

Opinions change; emotions change; times change. But God's Word never, ever, ever changes. And God has a purpose for every word it contains.

As a woman, I love, need, and long for security, and I tend to find my security in certainties (job, location, relationships, etc.). But what greater certainty is there than the promise that when God's Word goes out, it returns to Him, having accomplished the purpose for which He sent it?

So why would we seek our answers, our comfort, our joy anywhere else? His Word contains all of these—and more!

—BLH

Today's promise:
God's Word *will* accomplish its purpose!

# JANUARY 17

Ephesians 6:2–3, NASB:
"Honor your father and mother (which is the first commandment with a promise), so that it may be well with you, and that you may live long on the earth."

---

One of the national television stations in the US is known for recognizing when someone reaches his or her milestone one-hundredth birthday! It is indeed a day to be celebrated! I particularly enjoy listening for the person's answer to the question: "To what do you attribute your long life?"

The answers regarding the source of their longevity vary greatly and include replies such as:

"I love to garden/golf/walk, so I'm outside every day."
"I drink root beer every night before I go to bed."
"I eat a square of chocolate every morning with my breakfast."

(Okay, I may or may not have made that last one up, but it sounds like something that may be good to try!)

My mom once asked her elderly friend the same question regarding *her* length of years. Her answer? "I honored my parents. And God always keeps His promises."

They're not perfect. They're not even always right. But they are your God-given or God-assigned parents, and He has commanded you to honor them through your respect, your kindness, your love, your words.

If the Lord allows me to live to one hundred, make sure you watch for me on the morning news! I'll be the one giving the glory to God for keeping His promise!

—BLH

Today's promise:
God *will* honor you for honoring your parents!

# JANUARY 18

Ephesians 6:16, NASB:
"In addition to all, taking up the shield of faith with which you will be able to extinguish all the flaming arrows of the evil one."

---

This summer we went to an indoor amusement center and played laser tag with one of our grandsons. We played against each other and against some other children who were in there at the same time. I kept wishing that the "gear" that was strapped around me were a little smaller. I kept getting "shot!" But that worked to my advantage as well, because I was able to "shoot" those around me for the same reason!

It's just the opposite with the shield of faith. As our faith grows, its capacity to deflect the flaming arrows of the evil one—which include temptation, doubt, wrong thoughts, unkind words, and all forms of sin—also grows!

A wonderful aspect of this promise is that it is sure and established: the shield of faith *will* protect us. As we grow in our knowledge of God, our faith in Who He is and in His attributes and character qualities continues to grow and increases our ability to "extinguish all the flaming arrows of the evil one."

(The armor of God is clearly listed for us in Ephesians 6. I urge you to take some extra time today or sometime this week to read through each piece of the armor and notice its function.)

—BLH

Today's promise:
God *will* help you to use the shield of faith against temptation!

# JANUARY 19

Matthew 5:8, KJV:
"Blessed are the pure in heart: for they shall see God."

---

When aircraft are checked before each flight, a small sample of fuel is drained from the fuel tanks. This sample is visually inspected for its correctness (the right kind of fuel—which is color-coded, by the way), its purity, and for any water, dirt, or other contaminating substances that might be present. If any are found, they are removed so that the fuel is completely clean. Contaminated fuel can cause an engine to quit in flight.

Each day we need to check the contents of our hearts for contamination from sin and impure thoughts, motives, and desires. We must ask God to cleanse us of all that is unholy in our lives.

When our hearts are pure before God, nothing will obstruct our view of Him.

—JGH

Today's promise:
God *will* cleanse you from sin!

# JANUARY 20

Jeremiah 32:17, KJV:
"Ah Lord God! behold, thou hast made the heaven and the earth
by thy great power and stretched out arm,
and there is nothing too hard for thee."

---

This verse contains one of the most familiar and most frequently quoted promises from and about God: that *nothing* is too hard for Him! Think of what you're facing on this day, in this month, in this year. Does it seem like there will never be a solution, an answer, a way through it or around it? *Nothing* is impossible for Him!

But let's wrap our minds around the magnitude of that truth by looking at the descriptions of God that precede it in this verse.

This amazing, all-powerful, more-than-enough God made "the heaven and the earth"—the entire earth—simply with His "great power" and by stretching out His arm. Stop and dwell on that for a moment, because the magnificence of that power is more than we can truly comprehend.

So why—*why*—would we doubt that He can take care of our problem or supply our needs? Why would we question His ability to answer our prayers, regardless of the enormity of the situation?

*Nothing* is too hard for God!

—BLH

Today's promise:
God *can* do *anything*—*nothing* is too hard for Him!

# JANUARY 21

Psalm 16:11, NKJV:
"You will show me the path of life;
In Your presence is fullness of joy;
At Your right hand are pleasures forevermore."

---

Through the psalmist's words, God promises three wonderful truths in this verse:

1. God will show us the path to take.

One of the ways He does this is through His Word, as stated in Psalm 119:105 (NKJV): "Your word is a lamp to my feet
And a light to my path."

2. There is fullness of joy in God's presence.

True joy—which is so much deeper and greater than mere happiness—comes from God. "May the God of hope fill you with all joy and peace in believing, so that by the power of the Holy Spirit you may abound in hope" (Romans 15:13, ESV).

3. At the right hand of God there are pleasures forevermore.

Think about this one for a moment. The eternal pleasures we should be living for in the present are precisely at the right hand of God, because that is where Jesus resides! Colossians 3:1 (NKJV): "If then you were raised with Christ, seek those things which are above, where Christ is, sitting at the right hand of God."

Three amazing truths. Three blessed promises!

—BLH

Today's promise:
God *will* show you the path and give you joy and eternal pleasures!

# JANUARY 22

Psalm 55:22, AMP:
"Cast your burden on the Lord [release it] and He will sustain and uphold you; He will never allow the righteous to be shaken (slip, fall, fail)."

---

Life has plenty of burdens, and they come in all shapes and sizes. They can be single or multiple in number. They can be large or small in magnitude.

This promise presents the creator God of the universe in all His omnipotence, omniscience, and omnipresence as the One Who will carry the weight of your burden and uphold you in the process.

Whatever it is, God is bigger. And He is enough.

—JGH

Today's promise:
God *will* sustain and uphold you!

# JANUARY 23

Psalm 27:5, ESV:
"For he will hide me in his shelter in the day of trouble;
he will conceal me under the cover of his tent;
he will lift me high upon a rock."

———

"The day of trouble" looks different for each of us. For some, it may just mean a bad day; for others, relationship changes or strife may be the setting. For still others, death—or the diagnosis that will lead to its coming sooner than we thought—will be the picture that comes to mind. But trouble is troublesome—no matter *what* the trouble is!

God's promises in this verse should bring us great comfort and offer us the hope of strength. When we think of hiding or concealing something, it's usually because we're afraid and don't want what's after us to find us. Here, God is standing between us and the trouble so that it cannot touch us with the full force of its intended harm.

It doesn't mean that trouble won't come. It will.

But when trouble comes, there is no safer place to be than with Him!

—BLH

Today's promise:
God *will* protect you in the day of trouble!

# JANUARY 24

1 Thessalonians 5:24, AMP:
"Faithful and absolutely trustworthy is He who is calling you [to Himself for your salvation], and He will do it [He will fulfill His call by making you holy, guarding you, watching over you, and protecting you as His own]."

---

Today's promise springs out of the truth-promise that God is "faithful and absolutely trustworthy!" That truth is more than enough to carry you through the day.

But the infinite Giver of all good things promises that He will not only call you to salvation but will fulfill that call by doing the following (each taken from the AMP, as shown above):

- ➢ He will make you holy.
- ➢ He will guard you.
- ➢ He will watch over you.
- ➢ He will protect you as His own.

—BLH

Today's promise:
God *will* fulfill His call on your life!

# JANUARY 25

Luke 16:17, AMP:
"Yet it is easier for heaven and earth to pass away than for a single stroke of a letter of the Law to fail and become void."

---

Maybe it's the writer in me, maybe it's the perfectionist, but I don't like pencils. They're too "if-y." They come with erasers for a reason. On the rare occasion that I write anything other than a hastily numbered shopping list with a pencil, I feel as if I know that the plans will probably change, so I'm making provision for that from the start. But I want security. I want certainty. I want to *know* what will happen.

I want the schedule, the plans, the list written in ink.

This morning I read the oft-quoted reminder: "Don't doubt in the dark what God has shown you in the light." As I pondered the depth of its simplicity, I was encouraged and comforted by the fact that God's schedules, plans, and lists are written in ink. He never changes. And because of that, He can be trusted to keep His word, His plans, and His promises.

—BLH

Today's promise:
God's Word will *never* fail!

# JANUARY 26

Psalm 91:1, AMP:
"He who dwells in the shelter of the Most High
will remain secure and rest in the shadow of the Almighty
[whose power no enemy can withstand]."

———

This promise verse is overflowing with wonderful truths:

1. As God's child, you get to dwell in His shelter!

2. This is not just any shelter; it's the shelter of the Most High!

3. You will remain securely there!

4. You will rest in the shadow that His shelter provides!

5. If any of the things considered to be your enemies try to attack you there, they won't be able to withstand His power!

—BLH

Today's promise:
God *will* provide security for you!

# JANUARY 27

Psalm 46:10, ESV:
"Be still, and know that I am God.
I will be exalted among the nations,
I will be exalted in the earth!"

---

When speaking with one of my sisters about how God was working in my heart, I spoke of a renewed knowledge of the power of prayer. In her reply, she shared an important reminder through the following illustration [I have presented the true story as if in her words, for the sake of condensing our conversation that day]:

"When I was in England, touring the palace, we were reminded of an important element of protocol. When someone receives an audience with the queen, he or she doesn't walk in, greet the queen, and begin stating his or her request or offering comments. The person who is privileged to be there must begin by listening. The queen must always speak first."

Too often I begin my God-and-I-Time with my prayer list. I enter my time of prayer with sincere and appropriate petitions on behalf of myself and others, forgetting that I must first listen. The King of kings has given me His own unchanging words of truth, guidance, teaching, admonition, and love, forever recorded in the Bible. He wants me to read them, to know them, to live them—to listen. It seems that the proper order should be: He speaks, I listen, and in prayer, I respond with exaltation.

We must sit at the feet of Jesus and listen.

Because the King must always speak first.

—BLH

Today's promise:
God *will* be exalted when you listen and learn!

# JANUARY 28

2 Samuel 22:31, NKJV:
"As for God, His way is perfect; the word of the Lord is proven;
He is a shield to all who trust in Him."

---

I've never known someone who was perfect—without fault or error in his or her way of living. I've never known someone whose speech was totally reliable—entirely without sin. I've never known someone who was absolutely able to protect others—without some form of failure or inability.

But today's truth-promise describes our incredible God: perfect in His person, proven in His speech, and trustworthy in His protection!

—JGH

Today's promise:
Your perfect God *will always* be trustworthy!

# JANUARY 29

Ephesians 3:20, KJV:
"Now unto him that is able to do exceeding abundantly above all that we ask or think, according to the power that worketh in us."

---

The last airplane I flew was a big one. Its gross takeoff weight was 509,000 pounds! Passengers often asked, "How is it even possible to lift all that weight and fly so quickly?"

I would reply, "It's the powerful engines. Each develops twenty-seven thousand horsepower per engine on takeoff."

Our truth-promise today reminds us that we need His power working in us. We cannot face the day, the problem, or the task without His great strength. When we're all prayed-out, unable to ask or even think about what God can or might do, His power works exceedingly within us!

—JGH

Today's promise:
God *will* do more than you can even ask Him!

# JANUARY 30

Psalm 145:9, KJV:
"The Lord is good to all:
and his tender mercies are over all his works."

---

My husband's friend Ken is a godly, hardworking man with a heart of gold, and his heartfelt joy (even in the midst of difficult times) can make even the gruffest of men break into a grin. He loves to chop wood in his free time, and Joe and I envy his multiple, evenly chopped stacks of firewood. Ken is a true Southerner, and his Southern drawl is definitely on the "twang" end of the spectrum!

Several months ago now, Joe was talking to Ken on his way out of church. As the conversation was ending, Joe said, "God is good, Ken."

Without skipping a beat, and in his wonderfully authentic twang, Ken replied, "Joe, He just can't he'p it."

Sometimes we wonder in amazement that a holy, perfect, all-knowing God could love us; that the wise, powerful, creator of the universe could care about our simple needs and our desires; and that the merciful, grace-giving, wonderful Savior could forgive the sins that we feel are unforgivable.

But it's His nature. It's who He is. He just can't he'p it!

—BLH

Today's promise:
God *will be* always and only good!

# JANUARY 31

Job 23:10, AMP:
"But He knows the way that I take [and He pays attention to it].
When He has tried me, I will come forth
as [refined] gold [pure and luminous]."

---

The Amplified Bible brings to light the fact that God not only knows your path; He "pays attention to it!" He's there!

The fact that He is there—watching, leading, guiding, protecting, providing, etc.—can bring you great comfort when those refining times heat up. You can know that He has a purpose: to refine your life into "pure and luminous" gold!

No, while the fires of testing are surrounding you, it's not fun. It's not easy to see the desired end result. But it is imperative to remember His promise: He has entrusted this trial to you so that you will be stronger, wiser, better for having gone through it."

—BLH

Today's promise:
God *will* use the trials that come for your good and His glory!

# FEBRUARY 1

Deuteronomy 4:29, ESV:
"But from there you will seek the Lord your God
and you will find him, if you search after him with all your heart
and with all your soul."

---

Too often I flippantly read through verses like this one and halfheartedly commit to seeking after the things of God with *all* my heart and *all* my soul. Ironic, isn't it? Actually, it's sad, and I share it to my shame.

Friends, if we were truly searching after God with all of our hearts and all of our souls, our homes, churches, communities, towns, etc. would be transformed beyond recognition! I know this is true, because God promised that the end result of such activity would be that we would find Him!

Wouldn't that be amazing—to find and live out the very heart of our great God? Let's determine today to be world-changers, not because of our greatness, but because we have searched for God and have found Him!

—BLH

Today's promise:
You *will* find the heart of God if you search for Him!

# FEBRUARY 2

Isaiah 43:2, NKJV:
"When you pass through the waters, I will be with you;
And through the rivers, they shall not overflow you.
When you walk through the fire, you shall not be burned,
nor shall the flame scorch you."

---

On January 1, we looked at the fact that God *cannot* lie. I think that's why, in today's promise, He doesn't say, "*If* you pass through the waters...." He is honest with us and says, "*When*...." In other words, at some point, we *will* be entrusted with a trial, a change, a crisis, during which we will need to know that He is with us.

Think of Daniel as he headed into the den of hungry lions. He didn't wonder if God would protect him. He didn't wonder if God, Who might choose *not* to spare his life, would be there beside him, comforting him on his journey into death. No. He had come to know God so intimately that when the trials came, he didn't have to have a crash course in trust. It was already in place.

That's what God is doing in this verse. He is providing us with a promise that lets us know ahead of time that *when* these things come into our lives, He will be there!

—BLH

Today's promise:
When trials come, God *will* be with you!

# FEBRUARY 3

John 3:16, KJV:
"For God so loved the world, that he gave his only begotten Son,
that whosoever believeth in him should not perish,
but have everlasting life."

---

Just as finite life gives birth to finite life, infinite life gives birth to infinite life.

God's infinite love caused Him to give His only Son to pay sin's penalty—death.

This penalty was a debt we owed but couldn't pay. All who trust in Christ, God's Son, as Savior are not lost and do not perish but receive eternal and everlasting life!

—JGH

Today's promise:
You *can* receive the gift of eternal life through Christ, God's Son.

# FEBRUARY 4

Isaiah 41:10, AMP:
"Do not fear [anything], for I am with you;
Do not be afraid, for I am your God.
I will strengthen you, be assured I will help you;
I will certainly take hold of you with My righteous right hand
[a hand of justice, of power, of victory, of salvation]."

---

When my friend Rachel was a little girl, she would sweetly quote the King James version of this verse, which uses the word *yea* (as in, "indeed He will"). However, Rachel said it as only a four-year-old could, but in the way that we all should think of it: "Fear thou not; for I am with thee: be not dismayed; for I am thy God: I will strengthen thee; yea [only here, Rachel would shout, 'Yay!'], I will help thee; yea [yet another, 'Yay!'], I will uphold thee with the right hand of my righteousness."

If the promises in this verse don't cause your heart to shout a resounding, "Yay!" then read them again and again until they do!

God's multiple promises in this verse all fit under His statement, "I am with you."

- ➢ Because God is with you, you have His strength!
- ➢ Because God is with you, He will help you!
- ➢ Because God is with you, He will hold you up with His right hand!
    - o His right hand is a hand of justice.
    - o His right hand is a hand of power.
    - o His right hand is a hand of victory.
    - o His right hand is a hand of salvation.

—BLH

Today's promise:
God *will* be with you to strengthen, help, and uphold you!

# FEBRUARY 5

Psalm 55:17, NKJV:
"Evening and morning and at noon I will pray,
and cry aloud, and He shall hear my voice."

---

My dad, now worshiping God from his eternal home in heaven, signed most of his letters to me with the reference to this verse. On this day that commemorates his earthly birthday, which was February 5, 1925, I am again comforted by the truths of this verse and admonished by its reminders as well.

The psalmist knew that he could pray—talk directly to the Lord—at any time of the day or night. He didn't have to follow a ritual or a prescribed routine. He could simply "cry aloud," and God would hear his voice.

Wait. Did you catch that? God would hear. The holy God of heaven hears us! Prayer reaches the very ear of God and joins us to His heart.

Maintaining an atmosphere where prayer is free to voice its praise, its concerns, its needs, its longings, its admiration, its wonder is an all-day-long endeavor. But the results are amazing—He is listening. He hears.

—BLH

Today's promise:
God *will* hear your prayer!

# FEBRUARY 6

Philippians 1:6, NKJV:
"Being confident of this very thing, that He who has begun a good work in you will complete it until the day of Jesus Christ."

---

My dad used to admonish me by saying, "Finish the job." In today's promise verse, the apostle Paul wrote the Philippian church, stating that he was sure God was going to finish the work He began when they received Christ as Savior.

What work will God do in you and for you after you trust Christ? Romans 8:29 states that God has planned to conform you to the image of Christ.

Jude 24 (NKJV) declares that God is "able to keep you from stumbling, and to present you faultless before the presence of His glory with exceeding joy."

God wants you to be like Christ, and He will finish the work He started at the time of your salvation!

—JGH

Today's promise:
God *will* complete the work He began in you!

# FEBRUARY 7

Psalm 138:7, AMP:
"Though I walk in the midst of trouble, You will revive me;
You will stretch out Your hand against the wrath of my enemies,
and Your right hand will save me."

When the children of Israel crossed through the middle of the Red Sea on dry ground, the Angel of God put a cloudy pillar between them and the Egyptians who were chasing after them, thereby protecting them from their enemies. (See Exodus 14.) This was a beautiful example of what today's promise verse pictured: God stretching out His hand against the wrath of our enemies.

Don't you just love the fact that God doesn't just walk with us through our trials (see Isaiah 43:2), but when we reach the other side of the trial, He restores us, renews us, and revives us? How very like our generous, gracious, merciful God!

—BLH

Today's promise:
God *will* revive you!

# FEBRUARY 8

Psalm 71:20, NASB:
"You who have shown me many troubles and distresses
will revive me again, and will bring me up again
from the depths of the earth."

———

We confess. We enjoy watching the popular television shows in which skilled artisans take a seemingly broken-down home or object and either repurpose it or restore it to an even greater beauty, using the same wood to fill gaps in the walls and a new finish to restore the floors. Their work is inspirational, to say the least. Wouldn't it be great if we could "repair" our lives in the same way?

When love is lost (through death, divorce, a change of heart on one person's behalf, etc.), people often try to fill the "hole" with unlike elements: a sudden compulsion to work longer hours, food, shallow dating, spending money they may or may not have to spend, etc. But these surface elements will not bring true restoration to the soul.

The Lord longs to restore our lives, our souls, and those areas in which we have suffered a loss. Where do you long for restoration today? Allow God, in His timing and in His plan, to restore you and to strengthen the bridge between the present and the loss.

—BLH/JGH

Today's promise:
God *will* restore you and strengthen you!

# FEBRUARY 9

Jeremiah 17:14, KJV:
"Heal me, O Lord, and I shall be healed; save me,
and I shall be saved: for thou art my praise."

My mom was telling me about a man in her town who does home repairs. In her description of him, she said, "In this day and age, it's sad that you can't always trust someone to repair things the right way. But when this man fixes something, you know it's been fixed."

That's what this verse says to me—only in a more powerful way—about our great God. When He heals us, we're healed (whether here on earth or by taking us to heaven, where we will be fully healed)! When he saves us in the midst of trials, we are completely saved!

No wonder Jeremiah summed up his thoughts on these promises from God with the declaration that God was the sole object of his praise!

—BLII

Today's promise:
God will *completely* do whatever He does!

# FEBRUARY 10

Proverbs 16:3, NKJV:
"Commit your works to the Lord,
And your thoughts will be established."

---

I love calendars. There, I've said it. I feel much better already! But seriously, I could have a calendar in every room, on every device, and for every facet of my life, and I'd still want more. (FYI: I am pleased to share that I am getting this obsession under control and only have one on my phone, one in a book-style planner on my desk, and one on the wall!)

Because of my love for planning, it's easy for me to get caught up in the process—thereby wasting a lot of time—rather than following the instructions in the first half of this verse and claiming the promise from the second half.

So here's the best time-management tip I can share with you:

1. Commit the project, idea, day to the Lord.

2. Let Him keep His promise to guide you through planning and carrying out the steps to completion.

—BLH

Today's promise:
God *will* guide you when you commit your plans to Him!

# FEBRUARY 11

Psalm 57:10, KJV:
"For thy mercy is great unto the heavens,
and thy truth unto the clouds."

---

I love flying. I began flying airplanes at the age of fifteen—which was many years ago now! As pilots, we would often say that we had the best seat in the house!

Clouds, colors, stars, sunrises and sunsets, land patterns, mountains, and oceans—all this beauty passed right in front of the cockpits. Seeing this always reminded me of our creator God's vast and incredible creation.

But today's truth-promise also mentions God's mercy as being "great unto the heavens." How big are the heavens? Astronomers are still trying to reach the limits of the universe. But like the heavens, God's mercy is limitless.

God's truth is mentioned as reaching "unto the clouds." Like the clouds, God's truth stands, majestic and powerful.

—JGH

Today's promise:
God's mercy is *limitless*; His truth, *powerful*!

# FEBRUARY 12

Psalm 9:9–10, AMP:
"The Lord also will be a refuge and a stronghold for the oppressed,
a refuge in times of trouble; and those who know Your name
[who have experienced Your precious mercy]
will put their confident trust in You, for You, O Lord,
have not abandoned those who seek You."

---

Few of us can say that we truly have been oppressed in the way God's people were in the Old Testament. Few of us have had to flee our enemies, becoming refugees in times of trouble.

But we *have* experienced God's "precious mercy."

God doesn't use a scale of one to ten to determine how great our problem is, and He doesn't compare our trials to the trials that others are facing. Instead, he generously offers His love, mercy, and grace to those Who seek Him. In the process, we learn to "confidently trust" His promises!

—BLH

Today's promise:
God *will* be your refuge and stronghold!

# FEBRUARY 13

John 13:15, 17, NKJV:
"For I have given you an example, that you should do as I have done to you. If you know these things, blessed are you if you do them."

---

As an "ideas" person, I have a mind racing with great ideas. Putting them into action is a whole 'nother story! These verses with a truth-promise of God's blessing remind us that there is a difference between knowing what to do and actually doing it!

In this chapter, Christ gave His disciples a firsthand example of serving others. He washed their feet. No, this wasn't like the wonderfully pampering pedicures we can get at the nail salon down the street. These men had walked through dusty, dirty terrain, and on top of that, their feet probably didn't smell all that great because of it! Yet Jesus, the holy Son of God, stooped and washed their feet in an act of serving others.

He then reminded His closest followers that since they now knew what to do, they were to go and serve others.

But in the greatness of His character, He didn't just show them and then tell them to do it. He promised that they (and thereby, we, as readers and followers of these words He left for us) would be blessed for it.

—BLH

Today's promise:
God *will* bless you for doing what you know you should do!

# FEBRUARY 14

Jeremiah 31:3, ESV:
"I have loved you with an everlasting love;
therefore I have continued my faithfulness to you."

---

I did not marry for the first time until I was fifty-five years old. Yes, I had dated—often!—and yes, I desired marriage. But more than that, I desired for God to do whatever He desired to do in me and through me.

Many times during my many years with no spouse in my house, I read this verse, claiming its truth-promise of God's unfailing love and His faithfulness.

Interestingly, the joy, comfort, and security I found in this verse all those years continue to be mine, even after marriage. God's enduring love is still the love I treasure most. To know that He knows me better than anyone and still loves me—now that's a truth-promise I can claim daily!

—BLH

Today's promise:
God *will* faithfully and eternally love you!

# FEBRUARY 15

Isaiah 40:31, KJV:
"But they that wait upon the Lord shall renew their strength; they shall mount up with wings as eagles; they shall run, and not be weary; and they shall walk, and not faint."

---

For the next four days, we're going to look at four promises contained in the verse above, Isaiah 40:31: 1) We will be strengthened; 2) we will soar; 3) we will sprint; and 4) we will stand.

Each of these is contingent on our "waiting on the Lord." So what does that mean?

Waiting on the Lord means to trust on the Lord, to lean on Him, to rely on Him, and to hope in Him—instead of yourself or someone else. You have confidence that what He said, He will do. Therefore, because of the level of trust you know you can have in Him, you are willing to wait for His leading, His reply, His guidance.

—BLH/JGH

Today's promise:
God *will* bless you when you wait upon Him!

# FEBRUARY 16

Isaiah 40:31, KJV:
"But they that wait upon the Lord *shall renew their strength*; they shall mount up with wings as eagles; they shall run, and not be weary; and they shall walk, and not faint" (emphasis mine).

---

My most poignant experience in being strengthened by the Lord happened during my late wife's final hospitalization and illness. Though I was keenly burdened by her medical situation, my face radiated confidence and courage.

People would graciously ask, "How can you get through it?"

I would truthfully reply, "It's not my strength. It's the Lord's."

Just as He promised, He daily renewed my strength.

—JGH

Today's promise:
The Lord *will* renew your strength.

# FEBRUARY 17

Isaiah 40:31, KJV:
"But they that wait upon the Lord shall renew their strength; *they shall mount up with wings as eagles*; they shall run, and not be weary; and they shall walk, and not faint" (emphasis mine).

---

During my career with the airlines, I spent many hours in flight training and testing. These testing times were called "check rides," and it was easy to be overcome with "checkitis," the stress of being examined. I had to pass these check rides to continue my career.

Before each exam, I would pray and trust the Lord for His grace and wisdom. I would also ask others to pray for me.

Just as God promised, He enabled me to soar like an eagle—and He'll do the same for you!

—JGH

Today's promise:
God *will* help you to soar above your trials.

# FEBRUARY 18

Isaiah 40:31, KJV:
"But they that wait upon the Lord shall renew their strength; they shall mount up with wings as eagles; *they shall run, and not be weary*; and they shall walk, and not faint" (emphasis mine).

---

My brother, Scott, runs an eight-mile race with his daughters on Thanksgiving Day. Running is wearisome, even for the most avid of runners. In fact, Scott jokingly told me that there were times during the race when he thought the Lord just might call him home!

Running a race involves relying on training, effort, and endurance. Hebrews 12:1–3 compares our life to a race. We are to "run with patience the race that is set before us." Our focal point during this race of life is to be Christ, the Author and Finisher of our faith, Who will enable us and encourage us to persevere to the end.

Just as He promised, even though we are called upon to sprint during the race of life, we will not be weary.

—JGH

Today's promise:
God *will* empower you to run life's race and not grow weary.

# FEBRUARY 19

Isaiah 40:31, KJV:
"But they that wait upon the Lord shall renew their strength; they shall mount up with wings as eagles; they shall run, and not be weary; and *they shall walk, and not faint*" (emphasis mine).

---

God's Word pictures our lives as a race. A race can be fast (such as when we have many projects to do, have many areas of our lives needing attention at the same time, or have a complex task that requires ongoing effort). A slow race can be compared to times that seem dreary, boring, or tedious.

This verse speaks of running (sprinting) and not wearing out, but it also speaks of walking (stepping) and not fainting. He promises that we will remain standing until the race is done.

So whether life is fast-faced (sprint) or slow-paced (steps), God promises that we will receive grace to keep going!

—JGH

Today's promise:
God *will* enable you to stand strong until the race is over!

# FEBRUARY 20

Lamentations 3:22–23, ESV:
"The steadfast love of the Lord never ceases;
his mercies never come to an end; they are new every morning;
great is your faithfulness."

---

It's easy to cling to Christ when I am able to set aside possessions, people, position, and prestige and realize that Christ is all I truly have and all I truly need.

But then complacency, double-mindedness, and a lack of two-way communication with my loving, forgiving Creator set in. My crisis is resolved; my urgent need no longer exists; I'm settled back in to receiving the temporary salve of that which makes me feel better (about me), and my direction begins to shift. Yes, I'm still moving forward; I'm just moving in a different direction now—complacently wavering instead of fervently worshiping.

Then comes the reminder that there are fresh mercies for me to claim and apply today! His forgiveness is already there. He just opens His arms and with His unconditional love embraces my return as I confess my disobedience and repent of giving in to the distractions and the change in direction they produced.

And in that moment I choose Christ. I take His hand, determined through its strength and by His grace to retain my focus, to know Him more personally, and to walk gratefully beside Him.

—BLH

Today's promise:
God's steadfast love will *never* cease!

# FEBRUARY 21

Psalm 34:15, KJV:
"The eyes of the Lord are upon the righteous,
and his ears are open unto their cry."

---

When I first read today's truth-promise, I couldn't help but think of my sweet husband's frequent reminder to himself and to me: "Listen with both ears." Especially in today's fast-paced, technologically advanced world, it's easy for all of us to listen halfheartedly or to observe while listening to and watching other things around us.

Knowing that God is watching over us and listening with ears that are open to our heart's cry gives us great security. We have His full attention.

Does He have ours?

—BLH

Today's promise:
God *always* gives you His full attention!

# FEBRUARY 22

Psalm 117:2, KJV:
"For his merciful kindness is great toward us:
and the truth of the Lord endureth for ever. Praise ye the Lord."

---

I love that this little two-verse chapter contains a ginormous truth-promise!

We started this year of promise-related devotionals with the incredible promise to us that God *cannot* lie! That in itself is a promise among promises.

But today's promise adds a little "P.S." to that: His truth endures forever! It's not just good for a short time and then fades away. His truth never changes! What better foundation on which to build our direction, our choices, our lives!

"For the Lord is good; his mercy is everlasting; and his truth endureth to all generations" (Psalm 100:5, KJV).

—BLH

Today's promise:
God's truth *will* endure *forever*!

# FEBRUARY 23

Romans 8:28, KJV:
"And we know that all things work together for good to them that love God, to them who are the called according to his purpose."

---

Romans 8 is a tremendous chapter in the Bible. The word *things* is mentioned seven times in verses 28 through 39 (in the KJV). Paul lists these "things" to show us that our standing in Christ is secure.

Because there is no condemnation for those of us who are "in Christ" (see Romans 8:1), Paul can declare that nothing can separate us from the love of Christ (see Romans 8:38–39). He can also state that since God is for us (see Romans 8:31), no one can condemn us.

Therefore, we can confidently know that all things work together for our good and His glory!

—JGH

Today's promise:
God *will* work all things together for your good and His glory!

# FEBRUARY 24

Psalm 57:3, NKJV:
"He shall send from heaven and save me;
He reproaches the one who would swallow me up.
God shall send forth His mercy and His truth.

---

Flying out to the West Coast, I often flew near areas where forest fires were raging. It was incredible to see the huge smoke clouds and the vast scarred areas affected by these fires. Airplanes dropping fire suppressant were engaged—along with the heroic ground crews—in an effort to put out these fires.

In James 3:6, Scripture teaches that the power of the tongue is like a fire. This fiery speech from others can overwhelm and swallow us up. The psalmist tells us that like the airborne fire extinguishers, God will send His mercy and His truth from heaven to protect us.

—JGH

Today's promise:
God *will* protect you with His mercy and truth!

# FEBRUARY 25

Proverbs 10:4, NASB:
"Poor is he who works with a negligent hand,
but the hand of the diligent makes rich."

———

"Get-rich-quick" schemes and plans are all around us. Rarely are they wise options. I used to think these were new gimmicks that lazy people had invented to trick other lazy people into giving them money. But when reading this truth-promise in Proverbs, I realized that this problem has been around for literally thousands of years!

God uses the writer of this proverb to tell it like it is: If you don't work hard, you won't have financial gain; it you're diligent, you will have the financial gain to show for it. Period.

Finding the wisest and easiest way to do something isn't laziness. It's being a good steward of your time, talents, and resources. And it's often hard work to find the most efficient and cost-effective way to do or to produce something. But that's the diligence God is speaking of here.

And He promises to honor that!

—BLH

Today's promise:
God *will* honor your diligent work!

# FEBRUARY 26

1 John 2:25, KJV:
"And this is the promise that he hath promised us,
even eternal life."

---

Promises are special, because they are pledges or vows to do something. Their worth lies in the person who is doing the promising.

Think about what today's truth-promise says. Who is making this promise? It comes directly from our almighty God, Who is true, faithful, and eternal. Therefore, because of the One issuing this promise, we know that the promise of eternal life will be fulfilled.

Because God is true, the promise is true.
Because God is faithful, the promise will not fail.
Because God is eternal, the promise knows no end!

—JGH

Today's promise:
God's promises reflect His *holy character*!

# FEBRUARY 27

Nehemiah 8:10, KJV:
"Then he said unto them, 'Go your way, eat the fat, and drink the sweet, and send portions unto them for whom nothing is prepared: for this day is holy unto our Lord: neither be ye sorry; for the joy of the Lord is your strength.'"

---

Nehemiah chapter 8 began with the children of Israel asking Ezra, the priest (i.e., their spiritual leader), to read to them from the law of Moses. As he read to them, they were overcome with a sense of worship and of reverence for their holy God. They literally fell on their faces and wept in response to the recorded acts and words of God.

We are not told specifically whether these tears were over their sorrow for their sin or because they felt inadequate to keep the Scriptures that had been read to them. We only know that they wept when they heard the words read.

Whatever the cause, the truth-promise in verse 10 is still the answer: "the joy of the Lord is your strength."

When we feel incapable of doing what we know to be right, when we feel overwhelmed by the magnitude of the sins of our past or present, God reminds us—through these words recorded in Nehemiah—that the joy that can only come from a gracious, merciful, forgiving, loving God is more than enough to strengthen us to do the right thing!

—BLH

Today's promise:
The joy of the Lord *will* be your strength!

# FEBRUARY 28

Job 5:17, NKJV:
"Behold, happy is the man whom God corrects;
therefore do not despise the chastening of the Almighty."

---

God is not mean; He is merciful. When we trust Christ as personal Savior, God graciously causes us to be "born again" into His family. He becomes our heavenly Father, and as a good and loving Father, God deals with us as His children.

We *remain* in the family, because God deals with us as children, not as condemned sinners. God's discipline is corrective, not merely punishment for punishment's sake!

—JGH

Today's promise:
God will *lovingly* correct you as His child.

# MARCH 1

John 10:9–10, AMP:
"I am the Door; anyone who enters through Me will be saved [and will live forever], and will go in and out [freely], and find pasture (spiritual security). The thief comes only in order to steal and kill and destroy. I came that they may have and enjoy life, and have it in abundance [to the full, till it overflows]."

---

Our Lord Jesus Christ, Who is God (and Who cannot lie), makes very clear and simple statements about Who He is and what He does. In today's verse, He says that He is the Door—not just any door, but the door to salvation.

To be "saved" means to be completely and eternally delivered from the penalty of sin (which is eternal death). Salvation brings eternal life. Christ says to the one who would come to God through Him that he or she will live forever.

Interestingly, the thief comes, but he, the devil, doesn't get through the Door. The devil tries to do what he does: kill, steal, and destroy. But in and through Christ, we who have trusted Him are safe. Eternal life is abundant life that has no end!

—JGH

Today's promise:
Salvation in Christ is *abundant* and *eternal*!

# MARCH 2

Psalm 120:1, KJV:
"In my distress I cried unto the Lord, and he heard me."

———

An unbelieving friend of mine thinks it's odd that I even believe that God exists. Though she is never mean about her approach, she jokingly mocks my trust in the Lord, rolls her eyes at any mention of spiritual things, and thinks church is a waste of time when I could be enjoying a "lazy Sunday."

But when a crisis comes, she will quickly call or text, asking me if I would please "say a little prayer" on her behalf. Each time this happens (more often than you might think), I am reminded to keep praying for God to graciously open her eyes and draw her to Himself.

But I am also reminded that as His child, I can cry out to Him in times of distress, and He will hear me. This truth-promise assures me of that! There is great comfort and peace in knowing that my belief is not in a god who does not hear and who cannot care. My loving heavenly Father is real—and He is a caring, listening God!

—BLH

Today's promise:
God *is* real, and He *will* hear your cry!

# MARCH 3

Psalm 112:4, ESV:
"Light dawns in the darkness for the upright;
he is gracious, merciful, and righteous."

---

There are blessings—also known as benefits of happiness—to those who walk with God. We are in God's family through the new birth, by trusting Christ as our Savior. We have an eternal home in heaven with God. In our Savior, the Lord Jesus Christ, we have all the promises of God as "yes and amen." (See 2 Corinthians 1:20).

Because of our right standing with God, in Christ, we have insight in what otherwise may be a place of darkness. This insight comes through God's "gracious, merciful, and righteous" guidance.

—JGH

Today's promise:
God *will* give you wisdom and insight!

# MARCH 4

1 John 2:25, KJV:
"And this is the promise that he hath promised us,
even eternal life."

---

An old-time preacher used to say, "Simplicity is truth's most becoming garment." The context of today's verse declares that there are those who would try to fool believers by steering them away from the reality of God's gift of eternal life. (See 1 John 2:26, AMP.)

Christ Jesus promises eternal life. Therefore, as simple as it sounds, that life is eternal!

—JGH

Today's promise:
God's gift of eternal life truly is *eternal*!

# MARCH 5

2 Corinthians 5:17, NKJV:
"Therefore, if anyone is in Christ, he is a new creation; old things have passed away; behold, all things have become new."

---

Several words are used to describe a person who trusts Christ as Savior: he or she is said to be "born again"; the individual has "trusted Christ"; Scripture itself sometimes uses the word *converted* (meaning, to change).

Our truth-promise in 2 Corinthians 5 describes the changes in one's life when Christ becomes Savior. I knew such a person at the airline where I worked for many years. She heard the gospel through the personal witness of a coworker, accepted Christ as Savior, and began to change: she had new affections; the Word of God became precious to her; she made new relationships; God's people became her spiritual "family." In other words, all areas of her life seemed to make a complete turnaround. She began to live for God!

We who knew her could truly say that because of her salvation, she was a "new creation": there was a definite change in her heart and life!

—JGH

Today's promise:
God *will* change a converted heart!

# MARCH 6

Nahum 1:7, NKJV:
"The Lord is good, a stronghold in the day of trouble;
and He knows those who trust in Him."

---

We just got home from visiting a friend in the hospital. We spent most of our time there simply listening, caring, praying—as much for the patient as for the family member who was anxiously awaiting the diagnosis.

As we sat down to eat a late lunch and work on a few projects, our prayer was, "Lord, be that family's stronghold."

Because God is good (never unkind!), He is and always will be a stronghold (something strong to hold on to!) for those who need Him and who trust in Him.

—BLH/JGH

Today's promise:
God *will* be your stronghold!

# MARCH 7

James 4:6, AMP:
"But He gives us more and more grace [through the power of the Holy Spirit to defy sin and live an obedient life that reflects both our faith and our gratitude for our salvation]. Therefore, it says, 'God is opposed to the proud and haughty, but [continually] gives [the gift of] grace to the humble [who turn away from self-righteousness].'"

---

"But He giveth more grace" (KJV)...

...more grace than my undisciplined stewardship of my time and resources.

...more grace than my impatience—with others and with God's timing.

...more grace than my pride.

...more grace than I could ever be "perfect" enough to earn.

So today I claim that grace, and I find it to be generous—to be more! Because of His grace, He can, He did, and He will!

Sweet faith-friend, please cling to this thought today when you're feeling less than perfect, prone to wander, and weary of the constant struggles.

Nothing is greater than the greatness of His generous grace!

—BLH

Today's promise:
God *will* give "more grace!"

# MARCH 8

Psalm 25:4–5, NASB:
"Make me know Your ways, O Lord;
teach me Your paths. Lead me in Your truth and teach me,
For You are the God of my salvation; for You I wait all the day."

---

Several years ago now, my mom and I were headed from central Iowa, straight across the state to a town not far from the Nebraska border. My dad told us that it was a very easy route, and that there was only one little section to watch.

We were singing and laughing and talking, and apparently we didn't watch the road signs! Add to that the fact that my lack of good navigational direction is inherited from my mother, and you end up with two women who didn't even *know* they were lost!

To this day we still recall the moment when we simultaneously read a billboard that read: "Welcome to Eagleville, Missouri!" For those of you with the ability to know directions, no, we did not know we were going south instead of west! Oops!

Today's truth-promise reminds us that when we wait on His timing and His leading, God will lead us on the right path!

—BLH

Today's promise:
God *will* lead you on the right path!

# MARCH 9

Hebrews 10:23, KJV:
"Let us hold fast the profession of our faith without wavering; (for he is faithful that promised)."

---

Far too often we make promises in which, though the promise may say *yes*, it changes to *no*. Human promises can change and even fail.

God, Who cannot lie and Who does not change, makes promises that reflect His holy character. All the promises of salvation, the forgiveness of sin, and eternal life in His Son, the Lord Jesus Christ, are *yes* (see 2 Corinthians 1:20).

God's promises are certain, so we can claim them by faith, "without wavering!"

–JGH

Today's promise:
God *will* keep His promises!

# MARCH 10

John 10:28, AMP:
"And I give them eternal life, and they will never, ever [by any means] perish; and no one will ever snatch them out of My hand."

---

If you have received Christ as your Savior, you can't help but be strengthened and encouraged by His clear and commanding statements about your possession of eternal life. Eternal life is simply that—*eternal*!

But I also find comfort in the ending declaration of this verse: that no one is able to snatch the saved from Christ's hand. It reminds me of my wonderful dad, who used to hold my hand when I was a little boy. His grasp was firm, secure, and comforting. I knew that he would never let me go. Even sweeter is the promise from my heavenly Father in today's verse!

—JGH

Today's promise:
God gives *eternal life* to His children!

# MARCH 11

Matthew 28:18–20, NKJV:
"Go therefore and make disciples of all nations, baptizing them in the name of the Father and of the Son and of the Holy Spirit, teaching them to observe all that I have commanded you. And behold, I am with you always, to the end of the age."

---

In these verses, commonly known as the Great Commission, Christ gives a final assignment to His followers: they are to "make disciples of all nations" and teach them to be like Christ.

We are able to get from one country to the next quite easily in our modern world, but to those who were hearing these words directly from Jesus's mouth, the task seemed even more daunting to them than it does to us.

However, our great God never just tells us what to do and then walks away. He prepares us, equips us, and enables us to work toward accomplishing the goal.

And in keeping with Who He is, He adds the most amazing "Resource" of all—He is right there with us. And He always will be!

—BLH

Today's promise:
God *will* be with you!

# MARCH 12

Psalm 147:5, AMP:
"Great is our [majestic and mighty] Lord
and abundant in strength; His understanding
is inexhaustible [infinite, boundless]."

---

I had seen creeks, streams, ponds, rivers, and lakes. But it wasn't until I had seen the Atlantic Ocean that I had even a glimmer of the meaning of this verse.

As vast as the magnitude, power, and scope of the mighty ocean are, they pale in comparison to the greatness, abundant strength, and inexhaustible understanding of our God!

Today's truth-promise reminds us that these resources are ours to call upon, because the writer tells us that He is "*our* Lord"; therefore, His attributes are His generous gift to us!

—BLH

Today's promise:
God is *great*!

# MARCH 13

Psalm 126:6, KJV:
"He who continually goes forth weeping, bearing seed for sowing,
shall doubtless come again with rejoicing,
bringing his sheaves with him."

---

The Lord Jesus Christ, in the parable of the seed-sower (see Luke 8:5–15), declares that God's Word is like dispersed seed. The seed goes forth and accomplishes God's purpose for it.

Through the years, I have given out many gospel tracts (small brochures that tell about the Word of God) to people I have met. I have done this with the desire of giving the good news of the gospel to all. While I don't know how many of these tracts have guided their readers to become believers, I am joyfully confident that God will honor His Word and will use it to bring about the salvation of souls.

—JGH

Today's promise:
God's Word *will* bring about the salvation of souls!

# MARCH 14

Psalm 119:2, KJV:
"Blessed are they that keep his testimonies,
and that seek him with the whole heart."

---

God's blessings on us are shining through these promises each day, aren't they? Because of His love for us, God gave us His Word, the Bible, providing us with all that we need "for life and godliness." (See 2 Peter 1:3.)

It's one thing to have His Word. It's another thing to read His Word, and it's entirely something different to actually *do* what His Word teaches. That is what He blesses: a heart that seeks Him with such diligence that it lives out His Word!

—BLH

Today's promise:
God *will* bless you for living what His Word teaches you!

# MARCH 15

Proverbs 3:18, AMP:
"She is a tree of life to those who take hold of her,
And happy [blessed, considered fortunate, to be admired] is everyone who holds her tightly."

---

Today's truth-promise describes spiritual wisdom as a tree—"a tree of life." But how does a tree give life?

As humans, we breathe in oxygen and exhale carbon dioxide into the atmosphere. Plants, on the other hand, take in carbon dioxide and give off oxygen into the atmosphere. It's easy to see that God created trees and plants to give off the oxygen necessary to our lives.

In this verse, spiritual wisdom from God is symbolized by the tree, giving life and joy to our spirits. We must seek it diligently, soak it in, and utilize its blessings.

—JGH

Today's promise:
Spiritual wisdom *will* bring blessing!

# MARCH 16

John 1:16, NASB:
"For of His fullness we have all received,
and grace upon grace."

---

This truth-promise sounds quite, to use an old expression, "cut and dried." In other words, at first glance it seems very basic. But it contains a universe worth of blessing!

I think I'll just let the Amplified Bible break it down for us today, giving us a wonderfully overwhelming picture of grace on which to meditate:

> For out of His fullness [the *superabundance* of His grace and truth] we have all received grace upon grace [*spiritual blessing upon spiritual blessing, favor upon favor, and gift heaped upon gift*] (John 1:16, AMP, emphasis mine).

—BLH

Today's promise:
God *will* bestow on you a "superabundance of His grace!"

# MARCH 17

Psalm 18:30, NKJV:
"As for God, His way is perfect; the word of the Lord is proven;
He is a shield to all who trust in Him."

---

Today's truth-promise shows us three important truths about our great God:

- ➤ God's path — This is a lifestyle that accepts God, His values, and His purposes. (See Psalm 1:6.)

- ➤ God's precepts – His Word has been tested and has been proven true!

- ➤ God's protection – He is a shield for His children.

—JGH

Today's promise:
God's path, precepts, and protection are *yours* (as His child)!

# MARCH 18

Psalm 34:17, KJV:
"The righteous cry out, and the Lord hears,
And delivers them out of all their troubles."

---

The danger in providing an earthly illustration for a heavenly truth lies in the worry that my simple story will trivialize the magnitude of the truth in God's Word. So with that "disclaimer" stated, I'm going to share a quick story today that came to mind when I read the truth-promise in today's verse.

In my excitement to meet some friends for early morning coffee a few years ago, I was headed down the stairs in my apartment building and literally missed the first step completely. This mishap caused me to reach out for the side railing in order to keep from falling, but it was too late. I not only tumbled; I tumbled head over heels, landing on the entryway carpet at the foot of the stairs.

I called out to my neighbors, but no one came to help. I called again, this time by using their names, and this time I heard a faint, "I'll be there in a minute," before my neighbor stopped to brush her teeth and comb her hair (it was early in the morning, after all).

By the time she arrived several minutes later, I had realized that I could stand on my own, and that somehow I had survived the pretty intense fall with no injuries—other than a bruised ego!

So when I read today's verse and recalled my unplanned tumbling routine, I became all the more grateful for the truth that God hears my cry—*while* I am crying out—and then, in love, delivers me (according to His time, His plan, His will)!

—BLH

Today's promise:
God *will* hear your cry and deliver you!

# MARCH 19

Psalm 62:7, KJV:
"In God is my salvation and my glory:
the rock of my strength, and my refuge, is in God."

---

For salvation, people trust many things, including self, religion, or good works. All of these say, "Do," in order to be accepted by God.

Our salvation rests in God and God alone, and it says, "Done!"

Christ's fully finished work on the cross brings forgiveness of sin and justification before God. He is the only Source for true salvation, strength, and shelter.

—JGH

Today's promise:
God *will* be your salvation, your strength, and your shelter!

# MARCH 20

Psalm 119:160, NKJV:
"The entirety of Your word is truth,
And every one of Your righteous judgments endures forever."

---

I spent five years in college at a state university. The majority of my teachers were influenced by secular humanism and evolution. God just wasn't a part of any subject matter. According to their teaching, truth, if knowable at all, was temporary and elastic—subject to changes and revisions.

What a contrast there is between man's "truth" and God's Truth (His Word). All of God's Word is true and has *always* been right and true. Better still, it will *always* be true. It will never cease. It is eternal.

God's Word is worthy of our trust.

—JGH

Today's promise:
God's Word *will* endure forever!

# MARCH 21

James 1:17, NKJV:
"Every good gift and every perfect gift is from above,
and comes down from the Father of lights,
with whom there is no variation or shadow of turning."

---

While we often tend to focus on the good and perfect gifts that God talks about in this verse, today I want to look at the amazing truth-promise that with God (the Father of lights), there is not even a "*shadow* of turning!"

Additionally, we are told that there is no variation in Who He is. I am fascinated by the intricate color variations within the Pantone® color system. One tiny little drop of color added to an already existing color changes the color's name, number, and most importantly, appearance.

But with our amazing God there is not even a slight variation. He is *all* truth, *all* holiness, *all* righteousness, *all* love! And that will *never* change!

Now *that's* a good and perfect gift!

—BLH

Today's promise:
God will *never* change!

# MARCH 22

Psalm 62:2, AMP:
"He alone is my rock and my salvation, my defense
and my strong tower; I will not be shaken or disheartened."

---

I share the following true story not because I think I always have the right response—I don't! I share it because I put this verse to the test in my own life and found its truth-promise to be worthy of my trust.

The nurse came into the room and asked me to sit down in the chair next to her. As she described what the doctor had found in some of the preliminary testing, she concluded with this statement: "So you're going to need major surgery—soon."

I paused, silently and quickly thanked God for giving the physician clear test results, and then I replied in a calm tone, "So when shall we do this?"

Her reply? "Wow. You must have a really solid foundation. Most people I talk to about this fall apart or at least burst into tears."

I was able to share with her that I did *indeed* have a solid foundation—a solid Rock Who gave me His strength for whatever came my way. I added, "Don't get me wrong. I'm sure I'll cry at some point, but my foundation *is* strong. Now, when shall we schedule this?"

Friend, God is there for you. When He is your strong tower, you will *not* be shaken!

—BLH

Today's promise:
Because God is your Rock, you will *not* be shaken!

# MARCH 23

1 Corinthians 15:58, KJV:
"Therefore, my beloved brethren, be ye stedfast, unmoveable, always abounding in the work of the Lord, forasmuch as ye know that your labour is not in vain in the Lord."

---

Paul spent all of 1 Corinthians 15 declaring and describing the glorious truth of the resurrection from the dead by our Lord Jesus Christ.

Because Christ rose again from the dead, we will live again with Him. Because of His victory over death, we can rejoice! We must also remember that our work for the Lord should be done with excellence—because we know that it will not be useless and empty.

—JGH

Today's promise:
Your work for the Lord is *not* useless!

# MARCH 24

1 John 3:19–20, AMP:
"By this we will know [without any doubt] that we are of the truth, and will assure our heart and quiet our conscience before Him whenever our heart convicts us [in guilt]; for God is greater than our heart and He knows all things [nothing is hidden from Him because we are in His hands]."

———

Sometimes other people do this to us; sometimes we do it to ourselves—hang a past wrong action over our heads so that the guilt drapes down over us, prohibiting us from seeing the path on which the Lord wants to lead us.

But God knows all things; therefore, "nothing is hidden from Him." This is why He uses the Holy Spirit, dwelling within us, to prod us with conviction. Our hearts, sinful by their original nature, sometimes confuse the two: guilt and conviction.

That is why it's critical to understand the difference between self-created feelings of guilt and genuine conviction, which comes from the Holy Spirit, our Guide. It's also why I love the fact that this verse gifts us with a great truth-promise: "God is greater than our heart."

—BLH

Today's promise:
God *is* greater than your heart!

# MARCH 25

Psalm 3:5, KJV:
"I laid me down and slept; I awaked;
for the Lord sustained me."

———

When the psalmist David wrote this verse, he wasn't merely battling insomnia. He was fleeing from his son Absalom, who was literally planning to kill him!

Though there are, even today, areas of the world in which believers are martyred for their faith, I doubt that many—if any—of you reading this truth-promise today are hiding from children who are literally attempting to kill you (if so, call the authorities for help now!). But our Sovereign God, knowing that there would be times when we would feel the cares, pressures, and seemingly insurmountable burdens of this world crashing down upon us and around us, wanted us to know that He will sustain us.

Isn't it amazing that David so greatly trusted in the sustaining power of his God that he could sleep even in the midst of such horrendous circumstances? If God could sustain David in that situation—and He did!—then surely He can sustain us!

—BLH

Today's promise:
God *will* sustain you!

# MARCH 26

Isaiah 50:4, NKJV:
"The Lord God has given Me the tongue of the learned,
that I should know how to speak a word in season to him who is
weary. He awakens Me morning by morning,
He awakens My ear to hear as the learned."

---

All too frequently, we say the wrong thing. All too often we say the right thing in the wrong way. (See Proverbs 25:20.) Additionally, there are times when we just don't know *what* to say.

God can help us.

Today's truth-promise shows us that He can begin our day by giving us a teachable ear that can know what He is saying to us through His Word. He can then use those truths to help us speak timely and helpful words that will strengthen the weary.

—JGH

Today's promise:
God *will* give you the words to speak to the weary!

# MARCH 27

1 Timothy 1:17, NKJV:
"Now to the King eternal, immortal, invisible, to God who alone is wise, be honor and glory forever and ever. Amen."

———

You may look at this verse and wonder how it qualifies as a promise. But the truth that God is indeed "eternal, immortal, invisible" gives us the truth-promise that because of these attributes, His unique wisdom is available to us through His grace!

How can we not give "honor and glory forever and ever" to our amazing God after reading these attributes of His greatness?

—BLH

Today's promise:
God's wisdom is available to *you*!

# MARCH 28

Psalm 145:17, KJV:
"The Lord is righteous in all His ways, gracious in all His works."

---

I have become increasingly shy of using illustrations from other people or from using well-known individuals as examples. Invariably—and sadly—people who are lifted up as premier examples of right often are found to be doing wrong.

The blessed truth-promise in today's verse is in the twice-used little word: *all*. We can have confidence in the fact that God's righteousness will not change. There are no hidden secrets, no reasons not to exalt His name! All that He is, is right!

He is not only right in all that He is; He is gracious in everything that He does. Grace is a part of each action, each gift, and each answer to our prayers. Every time.

—BLH

Today's promise:
God *will not* change!

# MARCH 29

Psalm 116:15, AMP:
"Precious [and of great consequence] in the sight of the Lord is the death of His godly ones [so He watches over them]."

———

Death is not delightful. Death is not desirable. Yet, our merciful, gracious, loving, and almighty God specifically sees—and watches over—the death of His saints.

Their death is the "door" through which they enter a promised home in heaven. As seen in today's truth-promise, their death is important and of no light matter to God.

—JGH

Today's promise:
"The death of His godly ones" *matters* to God.

# MARCH 30

2 Corinthians 1:3–4, AMP:
"Blessed [gratefully praised and adored] be the God and Father of our Lord Jesus Christ, the Father of mercies and the God of all comfort, who comforts and encourages us in every trouble so that we will be able to comfort and encourage those who are in any kind of trouble, with the comfort with which we ourselves are comforted by God."

———

Many people reached out to me and said things like, "I'm praying for you," "I care," and "I'm here if you need to talk." Each was sincere in his or her offer, and I was thankful for every kind word following my broken engagement several years ago.

Then a friend who had also recently gone through a broken engagement called and asked if she could come over. I could hardly wait for her to arrive.

As we talked, she shared verse after verse that had helped her at the time of her sudden change in plans. She understood—in a way the others couldn't.

Not long after her visit another friend who had suffered an unexpected loss (of an unborn child) took me out for coffee and shared some of the verses that had been a comfort to her at the time of her loss. She also understood and could offer a listening ear that came from a heart of understanding.

God promised us comfort and encouragement and then reminded us to offer that same comfort and encouragement to others—because we best understand the joy of having received His comfort!

—BLH

Today's promise:
God *will* comfort and encourage you!

# MARCH 31

Acts 1:8, NKJV:
"But you shall receive power when the Holy Spirit has come upon you; and you shall be witnesses to Me in Jerusalem, and in all Judea and Samaria, and to the end of the earth."

---

The gospel is powerful. It can point people to a Savior Who will deliver them from an eternity in hell. It tells of one Who can give eternal life. It can change lives, because it points to the One Who changes hearts. It takes sinners and makes them fit for heaven.

Our promise for today is true today. In Acts 1:8, our Lord promised power to His followers to spread the gospel. The result is described in Acts 17:6: these followers "turned the world upside down!"

We have power in the Person of the Holy Spirit to tell others what has happened to us! Let's turn our world upside down with this wonderful good news!

—JGH

Today's promise:
The Holy Spirit *will* give you power to share the good news!

# APRIL 1

Hebrews 13:5, AMP:
"Let your character [your moral essence, your inner nature] be free from the love of money [shun greed—be financially ethical], being content with what you have; for He has said, 'I will never [under any circumstances] desert you [nor give you up nor leave you without support, nor will I in any degree leave you helpless], nor will I forsake or let you down or relax My hold on you [assuredly not]!'"

---

My friend Tara and I were laughing this morning about how easy it is to accumulate *stuff*—and how hard it is to get rid of it! (I was so relieved to find that I wasn't the only one with this problem!) It's definitely an ongoing goal to be rid of the excess.

As I read today's promise, I was prodded to think about *why* I hang on to things. Sometimes it's for sentimental reasons; sometimes it's because I paid a lot for it and feel guilty getting rid of it. But this verse reminded me that my security is not to be in *thing*s. I am to use wisely the money and material goods God gives me, but I am *not* to love them.

After his admonition, the writer shines a bright light on the *true* source of our security: the fact that God is a constant:

- ➢ He will never desert us.
- ➢ He will never forsake us.
- ➢ He will never let us down.
- ➢ He will never relax His hold on us!

What greater Source of security could there be?

—BLH

Today's promise:
God will *never* desert you!

# APRIL 2

Revelation 21:6, NKJV:
"And He said to me, "It is done! I am the Alpha and the Omega, the Beginning and the End. I will give of the fountain of the water of life freely to him who thirsts."

---

I love the language of God's Word. Here God, "the Beginning and the End" of all things, says that He will quench the thirst of thirsty people. Salvation is often pictured in God's Word as the "water of life."

Today's promise says that God will give salvation freely to all who are spiritually thirsty. In Isaiah 12:2, salvation itself is likened to a "well of water." This glorious fountain will never run dry!

—JGH

Today's promise:
God's fountain of life *will* quench the thirsty soul!

# APRIL 3

Psalm 73:26, NKJV:
"My flesh and my heart fail;
but God is the strength of my heart and my portion forever."

---

I rarely read this verse without thinking of my dear friend Betty (who was also my husband's first wife). Her precious heart tried so hard to overcome the illness that eventually overcame it in 2015.

For several years prior to her death, she would use this verse on the notes that she wrote to me. She knew that her physical heart was failing, despite every effort to the contrary. But she knew even more than that, that her spiritual heart received its strength from God. This meant that He was more than enough—forever!

Each of us, no matter our biological age, is getting older. Our bodies and the organs they contain will fail—unless Christ returns for us before they have the chance to do that! But our everlasting God will *never* fail!

—BLH

Today's promise:
God *will* be your strength forever!

# APRIL 4

1 Peter 1:23–25, KJV:
"Being born again, not of corruptible seed, but of incorruptible, by the word of God, which liveth and abideth for ever. For all flesh is as grass, and all the glory of man as the flower of grass. The grass withereth, and the flower thereof falleth away: but the word of the Lord endureth for ever. And this is the word which by the gospel is preached unto you."

---

This truth-promise is special to me, because it helped me to understand the eternal security that I have as a member of God's family by my new birth in Christ.

There is a biological principle of reproduction (called *biogenesis*) that says, "Like things give birth to like things." We could restate it as: "Finite life gives birth to finite life." Therefore, since today's verses state that God's Word lives forever and is like incorruptible seed, the life it gives by the new birth in Christ is also incorruptible and lives forever!

—JGH

Today's promise:
Your new birth in Christ *will* abide forever!

# APRIL 5

Mark 10:18, NKJV:
"So Jesus said to him, 'Why do you call Me good?
No one is good but One, that is, God.'"

———

A rich young man ran up to Jesus with a question: "Good Teacher, what shall I do that I may inherit eternal life?" (Mark 10:17, NKJV).

Jesus's answer to this young man is found in today's truth-promise. Our Lord was speaking truth, because He also told us in His Word: "I and my Father are one" (John 10:30, KJV). In John 14:9 (NKJV), Jesus said, "He who has seen Me has seen the Father." Therefore, today's verse is a wonderful reminder of the fact that Jesus and His good Father are one.

The opposite of *good* is obviously *bad*. Think of all the attributes and actions of God. There is nothing bad among them! Therefore, we can trust Him to always do what is good!

—JGH

Today's promise:
God *is* good!

# APRIL 6

Psalm 78:35, NKJV:
"They remembered that God was their rock,
the Most High God their redeemer."

---

The children of Israel complained and repented, and then they complained and repented some more. Sadly, we are very much like them.

In today's truth-promise, the psalmist was recalling how God had chosen to use some pretty harsh (but well-deserved) judgment to get the Israelites' attention. When He did this, they repented of their sins and "sought God earnestly" (Psalm 78:34, NKJV).

As they sought Him, they remembered that God was not only a powerful rock, providing them with physical blessings; He was also the One Who had redeemed them from the hands of their enemies.

How much better it would have been if they—and we—would never have forgotten these truths in the first place!

—BLH

Today's promise:
God *is* your rock and your redeemer!

# APRIL 7

Psalm 25:8, ESV:
"Good and upright is the Lord;
therefore he instructs sinners in the way."

---

Some men think that God created the universe and then left it alone to just run along—like a robot. However, today's truth-promise says that God is involved with people.

God is like a teacher. If the students are teachable, our upright God, in His goodness, will instruct sinners (those who are not walking in His way) in God's way.

—JGH

Today's promise:
God *is* good and upright!

# APRIL 8

1 Corinthians 1:9, AMP:
"God is faithful [He is reliable, trustworthy and ever true to His promise—He can be depended on],
and through Him you were called into fellowship with His Son, Jesus Christ our Lord."

---

The word *faithful* isn't one that we use very often. We may occasionally speak of a student being faithful to his or her studies. Every now and then we may describe someone as being faithful (or sadly, unfaithful) to his or her spouse. But I think our lack of familiarity with the depth of its meaning can prohibit us from seeing how phenomenal this truth-promise really is.

What an amazing sense of security is found in the fact that He is:

- reliable
- worthy of our trust
- true to His promise
- dependable

But there's an added blessing! Because God joined us into fellowship with His Son, we get to see His faithfulness firsthand—as His children.

—BLH

Today's promise:
God *is* faithful!

# APRIL 9

Psalm 37:39, KJV:
"But the salvation of the righteous is of the Lord: he is their strength in the time of trouble."

———

God's salvation means deliverance from sin's penalty, which is death. The God of salvation also gives strength in times of trouble, which *will* come.

No matter what question marks you are facing right now, God has promised to punctuate your day with the exclamation points of His strength!

We serve an almighty God, Whose person and promises are sure.

—JGH

Today's promise:
God *will* deliver you and strengthen you!

# APRIL 10

Acts 2:21, AMP:
"And it shall be that everyone who calls upon the name of the Lord [invoking, adoring, and worshiping the Lord Jesus] shall be saved (rescued spiritually)."

---

There was a time in my life when I really didn't know for sure that I was saved, though at age twelve I had made a profession of faith in Christ.

I should probably stop here and clarify what I mean when I use the word *saved*: it means that I am delivered from the penalty of my sin. That penalty, which was an eternity in hell, was paid by the precious blood of Jesus Christ when He died on the cross. (See the Introduction of this book if you desire more information about this.)

While I was in college, I heard an evangelist on TV preach the gospel. I sat at my desk at home and tearfully prayed, "God, if You didn't save me at age twelve, I want You to save me now!"

God answered that prayer.

He will do the same for you!

—JGH

Today's promise:
God *will* save you from sin if you call upon Him!

# APRIL 11

James 4:8, NASB:
"Draw near to God and He will draw near to you. Cleanse your hands, you sinners; and purify your hearts, you double-minded."

———

Joe and I wrote letters...with pens...on paper...and mailed them to each other...via a mailbox! Yes, it was old-fashioned, but it was a time-honored way for us to get to know each other better.

He would tell me something about his childhood years, and then he'd ask a question about mine and await my reply.

Then I'd write a response, stick it in the mailbox, and wait a few days for Joe's answers to *my* questions.

The more I knew about him, the closer I got to him—and vice versa. That knowledge grew into love, and that love led to a question to which I gave a committed, "Yes. A thousand times, yes." (See *Petals from the Basket [Book 3]* for more of that story!)

But the same is true of God. When I draw near to Him by reading His Word, I learn more about Him and love Him more. And here's the really cool part: He promises to draw near to me as well!

Herein is love.

—BLH

Today's promise:
God *will* draw near to you as you draw closer to Him!

# APRIL 12

Matthew 11:28, NKJV:
"Come to Me, all you who labor and are heavy laden, and I will give you rest."

---

We all have times when we are at our wit's end. Life seems crushing and heavy. These heavy burdens could have their source in people, things, circumstances, or even money.

Where can we find help for these burdensome cares of life? Our Lord Jesus Christ says, "Bring all your labor and heavy burdens to me. Tell me about them in prayer. Give them to me."

If you will do this, Christ—Who cannot lie, and Who is the creator of the universe—promises to give you help, true rest, and strength.

—JGH

Today's promise:
Christ *will* help you with your burden.

# APRIL 13

Psalm 11:7, AMP:
"For the Lord is [absolutely] righteous, He loves righteousness (virtue, morality, justice); the upright shall see His face."

---

As members of God's family, we need to learn what our heavenly Father loves and what He hates. God is angry with the wicked every day and will judge their ways. (See Psalm 7:11.)

But as His upright children, we will enjoy His care as He watches over us.

—JGH

Today's promise:
God, your righteous Father, *watches over you!*

# APRIL 14

Deuteronomy 32:4, NKJV:
"The Rock, his work is perfect, for all his ways are justice.
A God of faithfulness and without iniquity,
just and upright is he."

---

This truth-promise lists many qualities of our amazing God, but I want to guide your thoughts to just one of them today: "without iniquity."

Because "all have sinned" (see Romans 3:23), we will never know anyone about whom we can say, "He or she is without sin." However, this unique attribute of God makes all the other qualities in this verse possible. If God were to sin, He could not be:

- a Rock
- perfect
- just in all His ways
- faithful
- upright

His sinless nature assures us that He is reliable, trustworthy, and the keeper of every promise!

—BLH

Today's promise:
God is *without* sin!

# APRIL 15

Psalm 91:2, AMP:
"I will say of the Lord, 'He is my refuge and my fortress,
My God, in whom I trust
[with great confidence, and on whom I rely]!'"

———

When I took Spanish in high school, our teacher had us memorize Philippians 4:13 (KJV): "I can do all things through Christ which strengtheneth me." We had to learn it in both English and Spanish.

In the portion of the verse (in English) that says, "which strengtheneth me" (referring to Christ), the Spanish verse uses these words: "*que me fortalece,*" meaning: "who fortifies or strengthens me."

In my combined teenage naivete and arrogance, I was certain that it meant: "He is my fortress!" Similar, yes, but not when you're taking a test over the translation of the words!

Yet, I haven't been able to erase that thought from my mind—even after all these years. God, the strong fortress in Whom I can find refuge *does* fortify me and strengthen me. No matter how you reach the result, its truth never changes! And it's *muy bueno*!

—BLH

Today's promise:
God *is* your fortress!

# APRIL 16

Galatians 6:9, NASB:
"Let us not lose heart in doing good,
for in due time we will reap if we do not grow weary."

---

It's a pretty well-known fact with my friends that I'm an avid fan of Notre Dame football. (Go, Irish!) I'm loyal to my favorite team, regardless of whether they win or lose. (I didn't say I was happy, just loyal!) However, nothing can get me more riled up than watching a sporting event in which the team falls behind in points and then just gives up. Their momentum stops, their minds leave the game, and their team loses heart.

Baseball great Yogi Berra is often quoted for his remark: "It ain't over till it's over!" It's imperative to play—and to play hard—until the last vibration of the last note of the last whistle!

Not to belittle Scripture by comparing it to sports, but I needed a visual picture to help me with this verse. I think God is instructing us—coaching us, if you will—to keep giving our best, to keep moving forward, to keep making wise choices, because we will reap the benefits if we don't give up.

Keep plugging away. Take heart. Don't grow weary of striving for the goal, even if you grow weary in your striving.

—BLH

Today's promise:
In due time, you *will* reap the benefits of your labors!

# APRIL 17

John 6:47, KJV:
"Verily, verily, I say unto you,
'He that believeth on me hath everlasting life.'"

---

When the words *verily, verily* are used in Scripture, they stress the important subsequent statement made by the speaker. They could be restated, "Truly, truly" or, "Listen to me!"

Christ was addressing the unbelief of His listeners. He said that two kinds of people existed: believers and unbelievers. We could even say it this way: the "haves" and the "have nots!"

Those who *have not* believed on Him, *have not* eternal life. Those who *have* trusted Christ and *have* believed on Him to be their personal Savior *have*, right now, everlasting life.

That's great news! No wonder He wants everyone to hear it!

—JGH

Today's promise:
God gives *eternal life* to those who believe on His Son!

# APRIL 18

2 Corinthians 13:11, AMP:
"Finally, believers, rejoice! Be made complete [be what you should be], be comforted, be like-minded, live in peace [enjoy the spiritual well-being experienced by believers who walk closely with God]; and the God of love and peace [the source of lovingkindness] will be with you."

---

Good-byes in letters can take up much of the note, or they can be very brief. In today's promise, Paul is giving the Corinthians spiritual advice in the closing of his letter to them. He gives them a short list of "be"-attitudes:

- Be mature
- Be comforters and encouragers
- Be single-minded
- Be peaceable peacemakers

When these attitudes are present, God—Who is love and Who gives peace—will make these qualities abound in you.

—JGH

Today's promise:
God *will* give you His peace and love.

# APRIL 19

Psalm 119:137, KJV:
"Righteous art thou, O Lord, and upright are thy judgments."

---

*Consistency.* Consistency is a trait we appreciate and admire. It means: "holding to the same principles or actions" (*Webster's New World Dictionary*).

In flying, pilots are trained to a particular high standard of action and performance. Safety is strengthened when standard procedures are accomplished with consistency. Inconsistent adherence to well-developed safety procedures is a serious problem and is corrected through training and check-ride examinations.

Today's truth-promise reminds us that God's consistently right judgments result from His consistently righteous person.

—JGH

Today's promise:
God is *consistently* righteous!

# APRIL 20

Psalm 33:10–11, NKJV:
"The Lord brings the counsel of the nations to nothing;
He makes the plans of the peoples of no effect. The counsel of the Lord stands forever, the plans of His heart to all generations."

---

While I received good training in my secular field, I continually had to turn from the ideas and advice that I was receiving from ungodly sources. This counsel was not only anti-God; it was also frequently changing.

I rejoiced both then and now in today's truth-promise that God's Word—His thoughts and His counsel to us—are true, unchanging, and unending.

—JGH

Today's promise:
God's truth *will* stand forever!

# APRIL 21

Jeremiah 33:3, KJV:
"Call unto me, and I will answer thee, and show thee great and mighty things, which thou knowest not."

---

It was the second semester of my senior year of college, and I was struggling with organic chemistry. Someone from the dean's office called to ask why I hadn't registered for graduation. I didn't think I had enough credits. However, the caller stated that if I passed organic chemistry, I'd have enough credits to graduate!

At that same time, the airlines were hiring, and I needed a college degree to get the job. But first, I needed a grade of ninety-four percent or better on my second test out of three to pass this class. Be assured that I studied all night for that test, and that I studied diligently. I called out to the Lord to help me do my best and to pass that test. However, the test was hard, and I didn't finish it.

Three weeks later, the professor said, "Nobody finished the last test. So I'm going to give everyone a ninety-four percent—for averaging purposes—and not curve the grades the rest of the semester."

By the time the final exam rolled around, I had actually raised my grade by a full letter grade, and I passed the course!

One course. One test. One grade. My future career as a pilot hinged on this one pivotal moment.

I have since called this my "Jeremiah 33:3 experience!" No, when we call on the Lord, He doesn't always give us a passing grade, a good medical report, the financial amount that we're lacking. But He does promise to answer us and show us "great and mighty things" through His answer!

—JGH

Today's promise:
God *will* show you "great and mighty things" when He answers!

# APRIL 22

Psalm 34:8, AMP:
"O taste and see that the Lord [our God] is good;
How blessed [fortunate, prosperous, and favored by God]
is the man who takes refuge in Him."

---

We human beings are particularly finicky about what we eat. This pickiness begins in childhood and often continues into adulthood. We know and remember our likes and dislikes regarding food and beverages. Sometimes we have to convince ourselves that something tastes good, or we have to be admonished to try it in the first place: "Taste it—you'll like it!"

According to today's truth-promise, when we experience God's grace and mercy, it is like a pleasant taste that we can remember and can't wait to share with others!

—JGH

Today's promise:
God *is* good!

# APRIL 23

Isaiah 40:28, NKJV:
"Have you not known? Have you not heard?
The Lord is the everlasting God, the Creator of
the ends of the earth. He does not faint or grow weary;
his understanding is unsearchable."

---

"Don't you know that?" I've been asked that question before, as if I should have already known the answer. Isaiah asks a similar question in today's truth-promise, and then he provides some answers.

Since God is the everlasting creator God, He always was, is, and will be. He never tires, sleeps, or wears out.

Because God is God, we cannot fully comprehend Him or entirely understand His ways, but thankfully, He can understand us. And His understanding is infinite! (See Psalm 147:5.)

—JGH

Today's promise:
God's wisdom and understanding are *infinite*!

# APRIL 24

John 14:2–3, AMP:
"In My Father's house are many dwelling places. If it were not so,
I would have told you, because I am going there
to prepare a place for you. And if I go and prepare a place for you,
I will come back again and I will take you to Myself,
so that where I am you may be also."

---

I really have very little knowledge of what heaven will be like. Yes, I've read what the Scriptures say about it; yes, I've read a few of the well-recommended books on the topic. But I think that even the greatest of those descriptions will pale in comparison to one amazing fact:

*Jesus is there!*

No, seriously, let that sink in: *Jesus is there!*

We often console our own hearts with thoughts of sweet reunions with loved ones who have gone before us, somehow making it sound as if they are currently there, broom in hand, sweeping off the wraparound porch on our "family mansion," getting it ready for our arrival.

Oh friend, they are in the presence of *Jesus*! And if we are God's children—by grace alone, through faith alone in Christ alone—we will one day be there as well!

And then we will spend eternity thanking Him for keeping this promise and praising Him, because He is worthy!

—BLH

Today's promise:
Christ *will* return for God's children!

# APRIL 25

Psalm 121:3, KJV:
"He will not suffer thy foot to be moved:
he that keepeth thee will not slumber."

---

How many times in my life have I had the possibility of slipping or losing my step—both figuratively and literally? As I look back, I can see that God has kept my feet on solid ground, and through His constant presence—any time of the day or night—He has given me stability, despite life's trials, uncertainties, and difficulties.

These circumstances usually wearied me, wore me out, and caused me to fret and worry. But my great God, Who did not grow weary or even go to sleep, was always there—the entire time. Blessed promise!

—JGH

Today's promise:
God will *never* grow weary!

# APRIL 26

Proverbs 15:3, NASB:
"The eyes of the Lord are in every place,
Watching the evil and the good."

---

I love the fact that God is watching over me and watching out for me. Knowing that He knows right where I am (because He sees me) gives me an unmatched sense of security.

However, the fact that God sees all that I am doing—whether it's evil or good—causes me to tremble at times. In my moments of oh-so-human wrong choices, I think: "God saw that"; "God heard that."

And that is when I am thankful that He sees my bended knee and my broken heart and bestows His unfailing grace.

—BLH

Today's promise:
God *is* watching over you!

# APRIL 27

Proverbs 3:6, KJV:
"In all thy ways acknowledge him, and he shall direct thy paths."

---

Shortly after my first wife passed away, I asked close friends and family to pray with me for a helpmeet. Not long after that, God began to direct my heart to a long-time close friend of mine (and of my late wife). This friend had never married.

We began writing letters to each other and quickly realized that God was bringing us together. Each step we took toward each other was clearly God-directed. God gave us a sure love for each other, and we were married in 2016.

We both can say that letting God be God in our journey toward each other definitely allowed His promise of directing our steps to come to pass.

And I think you know that this dear friend who is now my wife is Brenda Lee Strohbehn Henderson!

—JGH

Today's promise:
God *will* direct your path!

# APRIL 28

Psalm 99:5, KJV:
"Exalt ye the Lord our God,
and worship at his footstool; for he is holy."

---

God's holiness is His essential attribute of absolute moral purity. Because He is holy, we must worship Him. Because He is holy, our worship should be done in a way that honors Him, not us.

Exalting Him as a holy God means to praise Him highly and to lift Him up in our acts of worship. Because He is holy and because His name is holy, our praise should be in keeping with the holiness of His name. (See Psalm 48:10.)

Because He is holy, we worship at His feet. Though we may not physically kneel at His footstool, our attitude should be one of reverential awe before Him. As today's truth-promise teaches, our worship should be worthy of His holiness.

—JGH

Today's promise:
God *is* holy.

# APRIL 29

John 16:13, KJV:
"Howbeit when he, the Spirit of truth, is come,
he will guide you into all truth...."

---

I attended a state university to obtain my college degree. In that secular-campus setting, I was confronted with all kinds of thinking—much of it relativistic and most of it without God.

I registered for philosophy as an elective course. We studied one philosopher after another, each declaring that he or she had discovered truth. I dropped the course, concluding that these thinkers were blind guides who were leading those who had already been blinded, never coming to the truth.

It was a great day in my life when I saw the Person of truth (Jesus Christ), the Word of truth (the Bible), and the Teacher of truth (the Holy Spirit).

This same Spirit of truth will guide you through your questions, give you the stability of thought that you long for, and strengthen you for the journey.

—JGH

Today's promise:
The Holy Spirit *will* guide you!

# APRIL 30

John 8:12, AMP:
"Once more Jesus addressed the crowd. He said, 'I am the Light of the world. He who follows Me will not walk in the darkness, but will have the Light of life.'"

---

Joe was recently working on a project to fix our grandfather clock. The location of the problem was in a dark spot inside the clock, so he asked me to shine a flashlight on the area so that his hands would be free to work with the intricacies of the inner workings.

Those without Christ often try to "fix" the inner workings of their hearts through good works, rituals, or some other means of achieving heaven through their own merits. However, they are working in darkness and cannot see that these methods will never be sufficient.

But in today's promise, Jesus told the crowd—and us—that He is the Light. When we choose to follow Christ, we no longer walk in darkness. The Light that gives us the life we long for can be found by grace alone through faith alone in Christ alone!

—BLH

Today's promise:
When you follow the Light, you *will* no longer walk in darkness!

# MAY 1

2 Timothy 3:16, NKJV:
"All Scripture is given by inspiration of God,
and is profitable for doctrine, for reproof, for correction,
for instruction in righteousness."

---

On my bookshelf is a large three-ring binder titled *Flight Operations Manual* (FOM). It's about two-and-a-half inches thick, with subject tabs that cover topics such as emergency procedures, weather, passengers, baggage and cargo, maintenance, reports and forms, etc. The list is extensive. As a pilot, I had to know, memorize, or at least know where to find the information necessary to conduct the flight. I carried this manual with me while on duty, which included having it by my side in the cockpit.

Thankfully, God has given us a similar "flight operations manual" in His written letter to us, the Bible. It contains the topics we need to know about (and apply) as we journey through life: the facts of creation, the sin of all humankind, God's plan of redemption through Christ, guidance for daily Christian living, etc.

Just as it was important for me to know and study the FOM, it is supremely important to read and study God's matchless, unchanging Word to equip us for godly living.

—JGH

Today's promise:
God's unchanging Word *is* profitable!

# MAY 2

Isaiah 65:24, KJV:
"And it shall come to pass, that before they call, I will answer; and while they are yet speaking, I will hear."

---

About a week after unexpectedly losing my job, I realized that I would have to upgrade my computer programs to enable me to prepare an updated resume and to begin the writing I felt compelled to do. However, funds were low—to say the least—and I had no guarantee of making any more money in the near future. This was not a frivolous desire. It was a need—no, it was a necessity. I prayed. Fervently—with sincere faith that God would answer.

And here's what my God did—just because He can:

That very afternoon I went to my mailbox and found a sweet card with a check enclosed. The senders stated that they knew I might have expenses during this time that I couldn't meet, and they hoped this check would help.

It was the exact amount that I needed for the software upgrade! The. Exact. Amount.

Yes, I was reminded that God answers prayer. But more than that, I was reminded that God didn't answer my prayer that day. He had actually answered it several days before, because my friends had mailed the check four days prior to my receiving it!

God reiterates this promise from Isaiah in Matthew 6:8 (KJV): "For your Father knoweth what things ye have need of, before ye ask him."

So ask Him!

—BLH

Today's promise:
God *will* have an answer waiting for you when you call on Him!

# MAY 3

Acts 4:12, NASB:
"And there is salvation in no one else; for there is
no other name under heaven that has been given among men
by which we must be saved."

---

In flying's early days, the idea was commonly accepted that pilots could and should fly in any kind of weather—just take off and settle down in the clouds, though they couldn't see the ground. Soon (and often with the tragic result of the pilot losing control of the airplane) the aviation industry realized that pilots could *not* rely on their natural sense of balance to keep the plane right-side-up in the clouds. Thus, the concept of "blind flying" (as it was originally called) came into practice.

Blind flying became known as "instrument flying." In instrument flying, the pilot is trained to completely ignore his or her sense of equilibrium and trust the instrument panel to tell him or her the balance, position, and direction of the flight. This trust in the instruments is absolute. The life of everyone aboard the plane completely depends on it. "Trust your instruments; don't believe your sense of balance!" flying instructors would preach. With training, practice, and experience, this trust became second nature and routine.

Trusting the flight instruments pictures the example of saving faith (trust) in Christ Jesus as personal Savior, the lesson clearly seen in today's truth-promise. Author Paul Chappell, in his book *Disciple*, writes: "Everyone trusts in something. Even atheists rely on their faith that God does *not* exist. Far more important than the quality or nature of our faith is the *object* of our faith. It is only when we trust in Jesus Christ that we find salvation, the forgiveness of our sins, and eternal life with Christ" (emphasis mine).

—JGH

Today's promise:
Christ is the *only* way to salvation!

# MAY 4

Isaiah 26:3, ESV:
"You keep him in perfect peace whose mind is stayed on you, because he trusts in you."

---

A young single woman recently asked me, "How did you know that Joe was *the one*?"

Without hesitating even a moment, I replied: "I trusted him, because I knew he trusted God."

That was really the answer in a nutshell, but I added: "If he didn't think God had wanted us together, he wouldn't have pursued me. But because he felt strongly that God wanted us to serve Him as husband and wife, he moved forward with the relationship. And I trusted Joe's trust in God."

When we truly trust God—because we know His unparalleled character, His unchanging attributes, and His unconditional love—our mind is fixed on Him. It doesn't waver. It *knows*.

And that knowledge of Who He is gives not only peace; it gives *perfect* peace that conquers doubts, fears, and distractions.

—BLH

Today's promise:
He *will* keep you in perfect peace.

# MAY 5

Psalm 100:5, KJV:
"For the Lord is good; his mercy is everlasting;
and his truth endureth to all generations."

---

My friend Judy is working hard to create a written record of her family's genealogy. She's uncovering interesting facts, informational data, and some fascinating stories about several generations of her ancestors.

As I think about the five months of promises we've looked at so far together, there have been several recurring themes. But of all of these, the one that has stood out to me the most is the fact (and therefore, the promise) that God in His very nature is eternal; therefore His attributes and His gifts to us also have no end.

We can see the magnitude of that fact in the truth-promise that concludes today's verse: "His truth endureth to *all* generations" (emphasis mine). God's infallible Word to our ancestors is the same unchanging Bible we read today. The promises He made to our great-great-great-great grandparents are still true for our generation—and for all generations yet to come!

—BLH

Today's promise:
God's Word *will* endure to all generations!

# MAY 6

Proverbs 3:12, NASB:
"For whom the Lord loves He reproves,
even as a father corrects the son in whom he delights."

---

When seatbelts first became standard parts in every car (and yes, I'm old enough to remember that!), people did *not* want to be required to wear them. Around that time, there was a television commercial encouraging people to "Buckle up!" One of the vignettes was of a couple sitting in the front seat of the car. The man, in the driver's seat, turned to the woman and asked her to wear her seatbelt. Her reply was something along the lines of, "Oh, he must really love me. He's making me wear my seatbelt."

It's perhaps a silly illustration of today's magnificent truth-promise, but the verse is pretty clear: because God loves us, He wants what is best for us, even if takes His correction to get us to that place.

—BLH

Today's promise:
Because God loves you, He *will* correct you!

# MAY 7

Psalm 107:1, ESV:
"Oh give thanks to the Lord, for he is good,
for his steadfast love endures forever!"

---

The truth-promise in this verse is clear to see: "His steadfast love endures forever!" The new mercies that He promises to give us every morning will never cease to show up!

But there's an important "non-promise" element in this verse that I want you to think about today. Because the Lord is good and because "His steadfast love endures forever," we are to thank Him. In this book are 365 devotional thoughts based on promises and truth-promises that were taken straight from God's Word. Have you stopped yet to thank Him for being a God Who cannot lie, Who keeps His promises—always?

If not, may I encourage you to join me today as I thank our good, mercy-giving God for the promises in His Word?

—BLH

Today's promise:
God's steadfast love *will* endure forever!

# MAY 8

Genesis 28:15, ESV:
"Behold, I am with you and will keep you wherever you go, and will bring you back to this land. For I will not leave you until I have done what I have promised you."

———

This is one of those promises that, although it was spoken (thousands of years ago) specifically to Jacob, still applies to us today. I say that because God reiterated His omnipresence in Hebrews 13:5, based on what He had promised Moses in Deuteronomy 31:6.

Because of that, I believe that He made this general promise to all of His children but reminded specific people of its truth right when they needed it.

Maybe He's doing that for you today!

—BLH

Today's promise:
God *will* be with you!

# MAY 9

Job 42:2, NASB:
"I know that You can do all things,
And that no purpose of Yours can be thwarted."

---

In today's truth-promise, Job said two things about God:

1. God knows everything.
2. God can do everything.

Knowing this, we must remember that God chooses what He will and will not do. This is why we should pray that His will—not ours—would be done, because His purposes cannot "be thwarted."

God's will is perfect, good, and acceptable. (See Romans 12:2.) We can talk to God about anything and trust Him for everything!

—JGH

Today's promise:
God *can* do all things!

# MAY 10

Psalm 56:9, NKJV:
"When I cry out to You, then my enemies will turn back; this I know, because God is for me."

---

Hasn't it been encouraging to read God's promises and to see them at work in our daily lives? The more we learn of God, the more we see that He is present, that He cares, and that He loves us unconditionally.

The writer of today's truth-promise had great faith that God would hear his cry and would turn back his enemies. How did he know this? Because he had every confidence in the promises of God and knew that God was for him—God was on his side!

This knowledge brings a confidence that allows us to say with the psalmist, "This I *know*."

—BLH

Today's promise:
God *is* on your side!

# MAY 11

Psalm 38:15, ESV:
"But for you, O Lord, do I wait;
it is you, O Lord my God, who will answer."

———

My dad used to tell me, "Son, you can always come talk with me."

That was a wonderful help to me from my earthly father, who always had an open door of communication. I could talk with him about anything at any time.

God invites us to talk with Him in prayer. Knowing that He will hear us gives us hope.

—JGH

Today's promise:
God *will* hear you when you pray!

# MAY 12

James 1:13, NASB:
"Let no one say when he is tempted,
'I am being tempted by God'; for God cannot be tempted by evil,
and He Himself does not tempt anyone."

---

I hadn't realized until recent years my natural tendency to blame others for my wrong choices. It's so easy, isn't it? When it's "so-and-so's influence" or "so-and-so's fault," I can allow myself to feel justified in my actions. I think, "It wasn't fair that he or she treated me this way, so it makes perfect sense that I had that wrong response."

James warns us in today's truth-promise not to blame God for the temptations we face. He doesn't tempt us. Period. He may allow things into our lives that test our faith, but He will never, ever tempt us to do wrong.

James continues by telling us the reason for this (which is the actual truth-promise): "for [because] God cannot be tempted by evil." What a wonderful truth. The God we serve will not be led away by temptation and therefore will not sin—ever!

—BLH

Today's promise:
God *cannot* be tempted by evil!

# MAY 13

Psalm 25:9, ESV:
"He leads the humble in what is right,
and teaches the humble his way."

---

God leads us by His example. He does what is right—always—so He shows us what that looks like. He also teaches us by His example. He says in Isaiah 30:21 (KJV): "This is the way, walk ye in it."

The apostle Paul showed us that we as humans have this same responsibility—not only to *follow* God's example but to *lead* by example. After teaching them not to be anxious (see Philippians 4:6) and to have their minds fixed on truth (see Philippians 4:8), in Philippians 4:9 (KJV) he tells the readers in Philippi, "Those things, which ye have both learned, and received, and heard, and seen in me, do: and the God of peace shall be with you."

—BLH

Today's promise:
God *will* lead you and teach you!

# MAY 14

Psalm 118:14, KJV:
"The Lord is my strength and song, and is become my salvation."

---

The psalmist says that God is and will be our "muscle and melody." It's true: we need strength for living the Christian life. Today's truth-promise tells us that God will be the strength that we need. But just how much strength do we need? God has more than enough, and He will give it to us!

This verse also tells us that God can be the melody in our lives. Songs cheer us and give us joy. Indeed, the joy of the Lord—not anyone or anything—will be our strength. (See Nehemiah 8:10.)

—JGH

Today's promise:
God *is* your strength and your song!

# MAY 15

Psalm 63:3, ESV:
"Because your steadfast love is better than life,
my lips will praise you."

---

The gift of God's unshakable, unchanging, unconditional love is better than life itself! That's not just a catchy expression—"better than life"—it's an overwhelming, phenomenal truth-promise!

I'm pretty fond of living, and I can honestly tell you that, outside of God's love, I know of nothing that I'd rather have than the ability to breathe and to be alive!

So how can I say that God's love is the one thing that is better than my very life? Because even after this life is over, God's love will still be there. That's why the psalmist concludes the verse with the natural response that I should have—both here on earth and when this life is over: to praise God with my lips!

—BLH

Today's promise:
God's "steadfast love is *better than life!*"

# MAY 16

Matthew 5:5, KJV:
"Blessed are the meek: for they shall inherit the earth."

---

We've all heard stories of children fighting over their inheritance from their parents. There is often tremendous anger, quarreling, and intense wrangling involved. Sometimes the inheritance is wasted and lost—in spite of all their efforts to the contrary.

God says that the meek—those who are mild, patient, and longsuffering (taken from Matthew 5:5, AMP)—will have an inheritance (a reward): the earth and, along with it, an abundance of peace, as seen in Psalm 37:11 (KJV): "But the meek shall inherit the earth; and shall delight themselves in the abundance of peace."

—JGH

Today's promise:
God *will* give peace to the meek.

## MAY 17

Hebrews 6:10, AMP:
"For God is not unjust so as to forget your work and the love which you have shown for His name in ministering to [the needs of] the saints (God's people), as you do."

---

Often when we help a friend by taking a meal, visiting him or her in the hospital, or helping that individual with a financial need, we do it in private. Sometimes it's because we don't want to embarrass the person or make him or her feel bad. Sometimes it's because the friend has asked us to keep the situation confidential. Sometimes it's just because it's fun to sneak a needed provision to someone and keep the attention away from ourselves.

But our all-wise, all-knowing, merciful, loving God sees the love we have shown and the work we have done for the sake of His name. He tells us in today's truth-promise that He is not unjust. He will remember that act of kindness, generosity, or caring—and He will bless us for it!

—BLH

Today's promise:
God *will* remember the love you show in His name.

# MAY 18

James 4:10, AMP:
"Humble yourselves [with an attitude of repentance and insignificance] in the presence of the Lord, and He will exalt you [He will lift you up, He will give you purpose]."

---

As a speech and music teacher whose job it was to train students to use their talents in an often very public way, I used to remind them of this truth: "Confidence is recognizing that God has given you the skills, talents, and abilities to accomplish His purpose through you. Arrogance is thinking that you had something to do with it!"

One of the most seemingly ironic elements of the Christian life is that as we become more humble, we gain more confidence. As we acknowledge our absolute need for the strength, mercy, and grace that can only from God, we do so because we believe that His promises are true. We know that He will enable and empower us to achieve the task He has entrusted to us.

As we see Him work to accomplish His work in us and through us, we are uplifted mentally, physically, and spiritually, strengthened in heart for the next task He sends our way.

Total reliance on God—the greatest manifestation of true humility.

—BLH

Today's promise:
God *will* lift up the humble!

# MAY 19

Psalm 119:172, NKJV:
"My tongue shall speak of Your word,
for all Your commandments are righteousness."

---

The women in my family have created a group text through which we notify each other of coupons, special discount codes, or out-of-the-ordinary sales at one our favorite stores. When we make use of the savings or coupon, we can't help but text everyone the story of the big savings we received, including the name of the item, its original price, and price we ended up paying after all of the discounts and special codes were applied!

This example should pale in comparison to the desire we are to have to speak the Word of God and share its truths. Why? Because of what today's truth-promise teaches us about God's Word: all of its commandments and teachings are righteous—without error.

And that's better than *any* department-store sale!

—BLH

Today's promise:
God's Word *is* righteous!

# MAY 20

Psalm 32:1, KJV:
"Blessed is he whose transgression is forgiven,
whose sin is covered."

---

I had a rather large debt that I knew would take me years and years to pay. When I received word that the debt had been forgiven—that I no longer owed the lender anything—imagine the feeling that came over me. I was literally dumbfounded, speechless, awestruck, and grateful—all at the same time! To this day I can't even fully wrap my mind around it.

Yet this is what Christ did—and so much more! I owed a debt for my sin, and my beloved Savior paid the price that I owed by shedding His precious blood on the cross of Calvary. God looked down on my sin, blotted out the debt that I owed, and said, "Forgiven."

The promise that I am blessed with this gift of forgiveness once again leaves me dumbfounded, speechless, awestruck, and grateful!

—BLH

Today's promise:
God *wants* to bless you with forgiveness!

# MAY 21

2 Corinthians 4:8, 9, 16, KJV:
"We are troubled on every side, yet not distressed;
we are perplexed, but not in despair;
persecuted, but not forsaken; cast down, but not destroyed;
for which cause we faint not; but though our outward man perish,
yet the inward man is renewed day by day."

---

A very godly friend first pointed out this verse to me when I was in college. He later went on to serve the Lord vocationally for many years on the mission field. When showing me this verse, he had recognized my troubled, perplexed, and cast-down state. The verse clearly described me.

Looking further into the chapter, at verse 16, I found serenity, clarity, and encouragement. I remembered that God's grace would be sufficient to renew me inwardly so that I could face outward trials!

—JGH

Today's promise:
God *will* renew your strength!

# MAY 22

1 Samuel 2:2, KJV:
"There is none holy as the Lord: for there is none beside thee: neither is there any rock like our God."

---

Dear Hannah prays her prayer in the way that only a godly mother can. She gives three truth-promises about our great God:

- ➤ Only our God is holy—absolutely morally pure.

- ➤ Only our God is God—no other gods exist.

- ➤ Only our God is a foundation—He is like none other.

I used to wonder about where God came from. As a child I thought, "Did He come from some super-race?"

But Hannah declares the truth: "There is none beside Thee."

Through His Word, God also answered my early childhood question. Isaiah 43:10–11 (NKJV) states: "'You are my witnesses,' declares the Lord, 'and my servant whom I have chosen, so that you may know and believe me and understand that I am he. Before me no god was formed, nor will there be one after me. I, even I, am the Lord, and apart from me there is no savior.'"

Question answered—and settled!

—JGH

Today's promise:
There is only *one* God!

# MAY 23

Philippians 2:13, NKJV:
"For it is God who works in you
both to will and to do for His good pleasure."

---

When we become believers of Jesus Christ, we have a changed outlook and a new motive for living: to serve God and to accomplish His purposes for our lives.

We often think that we have to live the Christian life and serve God completely in our own strength. However, today's truth-promise declares that God will motivate our wills and energize our actions to serve Him with joyful hearts.

—JGH

Today's promise:
God *will* work in you to accomplish His purpose!

# MAY 24

Psalm 51:17, ESV:
"The sacrifices of God are a broken spirit;
a broken and contrite heart, O God, you will not despise."

---

Let this thought grip your heart today: God will not despise a broken heart or a broken spirit.

He is not impressed with your empty words and broken promises. He is not pleased with your pharisaical, repetitious, mindless prayers that have no heart behind their words. In fact, in 1 Samuel 15:22 (ESV), He uses the writer of the verse to ask a rhetorical question: "Has the Lord as great delight in burnt offerings and sacrifices, as in obeying the voice of the Lord? Behold, to obey is better than sacrifice, and to listen than the fat of rams."

You can't fake it. You can't become a spiritual actress, thinking you can trick God into blessing you. He's too wise for that.

When the heart breaks over sin and the separation it brings from your loving heavenly Father, it is a brokenness that results in humble obedience. And God will not look down on that. He will honor it, bless it, and grant mercy and grace.

Every time.

—BLH

Today's promise:
God *will not* despise a heart that is broken over sin.

# MAY 25

Deuteronomy 4:23–24, NKJV:
"Take heed to yourselves, lest you forget the covenant of the Lord your God which He made with you, and make for yourselves a carved image in the form of anything which the Lord your God has forbidden you.
For the Lord your God is a consuming fire, a jealous God."

---

The children of Israel were given stern warnings against idolatry in worship. God demands for us to have undivided loyalty in our worship, which is to be for Him alone. (See Hebrews 12:28–29.)

God's righteous demand is that we be single-minded, not serving Him *and/or* something else. God's demands—in all things—are for our good and His glory.

—JGH

Today's promise:
God is a *jealous* God.

# MAY 26

Hebrews 12:2, NASB:
"Fixing our eyes on Jesus, the author and perfecter of faith, who for the joy set before Him endured the cross, despising the shame, and has sat down at the right hand of the throne of God."

---

Our faith begins with Christ. Ephesians 2:8 tells us that we do not originate our own faith with which to believe on Him: "It is the gift of God."

But today's truth-promise doesn't end there. It includes the fact that Christ, Who endured the agony of the cross and now reigns forever with God in heaven, is also the One Who "brings our faith to maturity" (AMP).

This. This is why we fix our eyes on Jesus and do not look away when tempted to gaze on temporal distractions.

Yes, my friend, Christ finishes what He begins!

—BLH

Today's promise:
Jesus is the *Author and Finisher* of your faith!

# MAY 27

Isaiah 43:25, KJV:
"I, even I, am he that blotteth out thy transgressions for mine own sake, and will not remember thy sins."

---

When Christ shed His blood on the cross, He bore our sins, nailing them to the cross. Scripture tells us of other actions the Lord takes with our sins:

- He removes them. (See Psalm 103:12.)

- He blots them out (as seen in today's truth-promise).

- He remembers our sins no more. (See Hebrews 8:12.)

- He casts our sins into the depths of the sea. (See Micah 7:18.)

But God's final action with our sins is the act of grace that literally brings me to tears of gratitude and worship. In Revelation 21:5 (KJV), God says, "I make all things new." John the apostle wrote in Revelation 21:1: "And I saw a new heaven and a new earth...." Then he adds: "and there was no more sea."

If there is no more sea, where are our sins?

They're gone!

—JGH

Today's promise:
God *has* blotted out your sins!

# MAY 28

Numbers 23:19, ESV:
"God is not man, that he should lie,
or a son of man, that he should change his mind.
Has he said, and will he not do it?
Or has he spoken, and will he not fulfill it?"

———

People sometimes tell lies. Sometimes they make promises that they wish they could retract. However, God is not like we are. He is truth itself; therefore, He will not lie.

Unlike us, God also will not change. If God says that He will help us, He will. If God says that He will provide, He will. If God says that He will guide, He will.

God's actions *will* equal His words.

—JGH

Today's promise:
God *will not* change His mind.

# MAY 29

Isaiah 26:4, KJV:
"Trust ye in the Lord for ever:
for in the Lord Jehovah is everlasting strength."

---

It amazes, delights, and yet also kind of saddens me to realize how many times God tells us in His Word to trust Him. It's so important to Him that He wants us to be sure to get it. But the part that makes me sad is that we have to be reminded so often to trust Him.

The truth-promise in today's verse is twofold:

- ➤ We can trust Him forever. This is not a one-time thing that we can be assured He will do. It's forever!

- ➤ We can trust Him forever because His strength never ends. It is everlasting!

—BLH

Today's promise:
God *is* worthy of your unending trust!

# MAY 30

Psalm 89:33, KJV:
"Nevertheless my lovingkindness will I not utterly take from him, nor suffer my faithfulness to fail."

---

The setting of this Psalm is from the life of King David and God's promises to him. But the truth-promise is also for us.

What a comfort it is to know that He will be faithful—no matter what we are facing, no matter what the diagnosis, no matter how shattered the earthly relationship may seem. He will be there. He won't withdraw His help.

Even when we think all hope is gone, God will not run away from us in our trials.

—BLH/JGH

Today's promise:
God's faithfulness will *never* fail!

# MAY 31

Philippians 4:6–7, NKJV:
"Be anxious for nothing, but in everything by prayer and supplication, with thanksgiving, let your requests be made known to God; and the peace of God, which surpasses all understanding, will guard your hearts and minds through Christ Jesus."

---

Paul was writing from a prison cell when he wrote these words to the believers in Philippi. The theme of his letter was Christian joy—that inner peace and contentment that only God can give, in spite of people, circumstances, and trials.

In today's promise, Paul's formula for inner serenity is in three parts:

1. Worry about nothing.

2. Pray and thank God for everything.

3. Receive God's peace about all things.

—JGH

Today's promise:
God *will* give you peace!

# JUNE 1

Psalm 91:14, KJV:
"Because he has set his love upon Me, therefore I will deliver him; I will set him on high, because he has known My name."

---

If some random person came up and asked to borrow my car, I would say no. If a friend asked, I'd probably hand her the keys. (Notice the word *probably*! I do have a few friends who should probably not be trusted with my keys!)

If a stranger handed me her Christmas list, I'd hand it back to her. If my family members handed me theirs, I'd joyfully provide what I could from the lists.

When I read today's promise, I can't help but be overcome with gratitude for the personal nature of our amazing God. He longs to have a relationship with us that is close, genuine, and lasting. When there is a bond between people, there are also the benefits of trust, love, and frequent interaction.

As you study the names of God—and I urge you to do that if you haven't already—you will see His character qualities revealed, thereby deepening your understanding of Who He is. Your love for Him will grow as your knowledge of Him increases!

—BLH

Today's promise:
God *will* honor His relationship with you!

# JUNE 2

John 16:33, KJV:
"These things I have spoken unto you, that in me ye might have peace. In the world ye shall have tribulation: but be of good cheer; I have overcome the world."

———

Today, I will prove your high school math teacher right: you *will* use math facts after high school!

If A > B, and B > C, then A > C.

While I would not want merely to compare Scripture with mathematical information, I think this math truth can help to portray the truth of John 16:33. Hear me out.

1. God is greater than this world and has overcome it. That's a fact about which there is no denying. (See 1 John 4:4 in addition to today's promise verse.) [A > B]

2. The world is greater than the tribulation it contains. [B > C]

3. Therefore, because of God's great power, He is greater than any tribulation that could come your way! [A > C]

No wonder we can "be of good cheer" and "have peace" today!

—BLH

Today's promise:
He *has overcome* the world (*and* its tribulations)!

# JUNE 3

Romans 11:33, KJV:
"O the depth of the riches both of the wisdom and knowledge of God! how unsearchable are his judgments, and his ways past finding out!"

---

Our God is not only God; He is a *great* God! Even today's truth-promise is simply incapable of fully expressing the greatness of our God.

Notice that there are exclamation points at the end of each statement in today's verse.

- ❖ God is inexpressibly great in His wisdom!

- ❖ God is inexpressibly great in His knowledge!

- ❖ God is inexpressibly great in His decisions and actions!

When describing our God, exclamation points are required!

—JGII

Today's promise:
God *is* inexpressibly great!

# JUNE 4

Exodus 14:13–14, ESV:
"And Moses said to the people, 'Fear not, stand firm, and see the salvation of the Lord, which he will work for you today.
For the Egyptians whom you see today, you shall never see again. The Lord will fight for you, and you have only to be silent.'"

---

I don't recall that my mom ever yelled at us. Instead, her voice grew softer when she wanted us to stop quarreling, be still, and listen. In like manner, as the children of Israel were being chased, literally, by the Egyptians who had enslaved them, Moses instructed them to "stand still."

They were frantic. Their emotions were getting the best of them, and they were inciting a "mob mentality": because the growing crowd of nervous complainers was growing, more were joining in, getting even more people all riled up.

However, Moses had listened to, learned from, and personally witnessed numerous acts of God by this time, and he knew that the key to keeping calm in the midst of uncertain change was to rely on the power of the almighty God. Moses could give the instructions of verse 13 because he believed the promise in verse 14.

The promise of this verse—"The Lord will fight for you"—was originally spoken in a specific setting for a specific time. But we often enter times when we grow frantic, listen to bad input from others, and are fearful of the outcome. The same God Who fought for the Israelites will fight for us!

—BLH

Today's promise:
The Lord *will* fight for you!

# JUNE 5

Psalm 103:12, KJV:
"As far as the east is from the west,
so far hath he removed our transgressions from us."

---

Geometry was one of my favorite classes in high school. Mr. Jenkins, my geometry teacher, loved both his subject and his students. When I think of today's truth-promise, I recall learning about lines and using arrows on the ends of those lines to signify that the lines extended into infinity in both directions. (Oh how I hope I got that right! High school was a long time ago!)

That's one of the first visual pictures I think of when I read this verse, assuring me that on that infinite line, the east will never meet the west, nor vice versa!

The evil one wants you to believe that you still carry the guilt of those sins—that you are not of any value to God because of them. But that brings two *rhetorical* questions to mind:

1. If your sins are that far away—and they are—why would you allow the "evil ick" (i.e., the devil) to keep them near with his accusations?

2. If you have no value to God, why would He have sent His precious and only Son to die on a cross in order to pay the penalty for your sins?

—BLH

Today's promise:
God *has removed* your sins!

# JUNE 6

Jeremiah 23:23–24, KJV:
"'Am I a God at hand,' saith the Lord, 'and not a God afar off? Can any hide himself in secret places that I shall not see him?' saith the Lord. 'Do not I fill heaven and earth?' saith the Lord."

---

Do you remember when you were a child and were, perhaps, up to no good? You would say to your friends, "Don't worry. My parents can't see us!"

You cannot run away from God or hide from Him! (See Genesis 16:13.)

Do you also remember being afraid in your room at night? Your parents would say, "Don't worry. We're in the room right next door."

In today's truth-promise God is describing Himself. He says that He is not far away; He is near.

Let these truths from God Himself bless you. Remember that God is near to hear you and to help you!

—JGH

Today's promise:
God *is* near!

# JUNE 7

2 Corinthians 9:10, NASB:
"Now He who supplies seed to the sower and bread for food will supply and multiply your seed for sowing and increase the harvest of your righteousness."

---

Giving to the Lord and His cause is a special privilege for all who follow Christ. God is able to supply the gift and bless the giver, multiplying the results of the gift given.

Not only can God enable you to give; He can magnify the impact and influence of those gifts to His work. This applies to anything that you give to the Lord: time, talents, treasures, etc.

—JGH

Today's promise:
God *will* bless the gifts you give to Him.

# JUNE 8

2 Chronicles 16:9, KJV:
"For the eyes of the Lord run to and fro throughout the whole earth, to show Himself strong on behalf of those whose heart is loyal to Him. In this you have done foolishly; therefore from now on you shall have wars."

———

During my career as an airline pilot, I carried two bags: one, an overnight bag with clothes and other essentials; the other, a heavy, black, flight-kit bag that carried maps and manuals. When I would board an airport parking-lot shuttle bus, I would have to lift those bags onto shelves, where they would stay during our short journey to or from the airport. I really didn't like "lugging luggage!"

Frequently, it seemed, someone would board the bus and have difficulty lifting his or her bags onto the shelves. I would watch for these opportunities to help and would offer my assistance if the need presented itself. The person could either refuse my help or accept it.

Today's truth-promise describes God's willingness to help. His infinite eyes see opportunities everywhere. But notice that, first, our hearts *must* be willing to accept His help.

—JGH

Today's promise:
God *will* show Himself strong!

# JUNE 9

1 Timothy 6:17, AMP:
"As for the rich in this present world, instruct them not to be conceited and arrogant, nor to set their hope on the uncertainty of riches, but on God, who richly and ceaselessly provides us with everything for our enjoyment."

---

Have you noticed that many of the promises and truth-promises include commandments, instructions, or warnings? Today's verse is one of those.

Timothy is reminding his readers—therefore, us—not to be arrogant about or overly confident in the ongoing existence of our earthly riches. He is not condemning the riches or the people who possess them. He is, however, warning us to maintain a right focus.

The right focus comes in the truth-promise itself: God "richly and ceaselessly" provides us with all that we need—and more! This is true no matter what our annual income may be. God's provision, unlike the existence of riches, is certain!

—BLH

Today's promise:
God "richly and ceaselessly" provides all that you need—*and more*!

# JUNE 10

Isaiah 30:18, AMP:
"Therefore the Lord waits [expectantly] and longs to be gracious to you, And therefore He waits on high to have compassion on you. For the Lord is a God of justice; blessed (happy, fortunate) are all those who long for Him [since He will never fail them]."

---

When I was growing up, I sometimes had to wait for my parents to help me with a task or project. They would always assure me of their willingness to help, but they would sometimes ask me to wait.

Today's promise describes God's apparent delays. His seeming inactivity on our behalf causes us to wait on Him. The verse also declares that God is gracious and always right.

He wants to help us, but it will be on *His* schedule, not ours.

—JGH

Today's promise:
God *longs* to be gracious to you!

# JUNE 11

Psalm 118:6, KJV:
"The Lord is on my side; I will not fear:
what can man do unto me?"

---

Parents can't "take sides" when their children argue. Children should experience unbiased love from their parents and have equivalent standing with them.

God, as our Father, is the same: He does not differentiate between sinners when it comes to His free gift of salvation. He offers His blessings to all who are His children.

But when it comes to siding with His children over those Who are His enemies, He (like any good earthly parent as well) *will* take sides. And He will always choose to side with His children!

—BLH

Today's promise:
The Lord *is* on your side!

# JUNE 12

1 Corinthians 8:6, NKJV:
"Yet for us there is one God, the Father, of whom are all things,
and we for Him; and one Lord Jesus Christ,
through whom are all things, and through whom we live."

---

Paul is writing to the Corinthians about idols, the other "gods" they once worshipped. We know what Paul and the Corinthian believers knew: that idols are dead gods.

He tells them that not all people know the only true God, Whom they know through Jesus Christ. Paul finally and clearly declares (as seen in today's truth-promise) that only one true God exists.

He concluded this thought by reminding the Corinthian believers (and all readers of these truths of Scripture) that they know God and are in God by their faith in Jesus Christ.

—JGH

Today's promise:
God is the *only* true and living God!

# JUNE 13

Acts 20:32, AMP:
"And now I commend you to God [placing you in His protective, loving care] and [I commend you] to the word of His grace [the counsel and promises of His unmerited favor]. His grace is able to build you up and to give you the [rightful] inheritance among all those who are sanctified [that is, among those who are set apart for God's purpose—all believers]."

---

The writer of these words, believed to be Luke (a physician), in closing his letter, states that God not only will protect His children, but He will provide the grace that only He can give. This alone is a great truth-promise for the initial readers of these words—and also for us, as readers of these words today.

But he doesn't stop there. Luke reminds us that God's blessings don't end when we leave this earth. God has an inheritance waiting for us in heaven. We—along with all who have trusted in Jesus Christ the Lord as their Savior—will be recipients of the privilege of praising and worshipping God for all eternity!

—BLH

Today's promise:
God *will* give you the inheritance of eternal life!

# JUNE 14

Isaiah 52:12, AMP:
"For you will not go out in a hurry [as when you left Egypt],
Nor will you go in flight [fleeing, as you did from the Egyptians];
For the Lord will go before you,
And the God of Israel will be your rear guard."

---

In the front of my Bible I have written the following (source unknown):

God is ahead – our Shepherd
God is behind – our Guard
God is beside – our Comfort
God is above – our Covering
God is below – our Foundation
God is within – our Life

"As the mountains are round about Jerusalem, so the Lord is round about his people from henceforth even for ever" (Psalm 125:2, KJV).

—JGH

Today's promise:
God *will* protect you on every side!

# JUNE 15

Psalm 62:5, AMP:
"For God alone my soul waits in silence and quietly submits to Him, for my hope is from Him."

---

When your hope is in God, trusting, waiting, and quietly submitting to His plans are natural byproducts.

When your hope is in God, you know that you need nothing else; your hope is in Him alone.

When your hope is in God, your soul can know true rest.

When your hope is in God, your desires will be His desires—they will be "from Him."

—BLH

Today's promise:
When your hope is in God, He *is* enough.

# JUNE 16

Romans 15:5, KJV:
"Now may the God of patience and comfort grant you to be like-minded toward one another, according to Christ Jesus."

---

How helpful and practical God's Word is to us! We have everything we need "that pertains to life and godliness" (see 2 Peter 1:3–4).

Today's truth-promise tells us two qualities that we need in our lives and in our relationships:

*Patience*, which is calmness and self-control (*Webster's New World Dictionary*), is a quality we don't naturally possess. We become impatient with seemingly everyone and everything.

*Comfort* is another trait that we need in our lives. Not only do we need to be comforted, but we need to be comforters of others.

God, Who graciously meets all our needs, promises to make us people of patience and comfort in our dealings with others.

—JGH

Today's promise:
God *is* the God of patience and comfort.

# JUNE 17

Acts 26:8, KJV:
"Why should it be thought a thing incredible with you, that God should raise the dead?"

---

Paul the apostle was a tremendous example of the grace of God. When standing before Agrippa, the ruler, he shared what God had done in his life. He asked, "Does it seem improbable that God would raise the dead?" He proceeded to tell King Agrippa that he, Paul, had seen the resurrected Lord.

Today's truth-promise asks a question in order to make a point. In view of all the other incredible things that God has done, it should *not* seem improbable for God to raise the dead!

—JGH

Today's promise:
God's power should *never* be a surprise to you!

# JUNE 18

Psalm 5:12, KJV:
"For You, O Lord, will bless the righteous;
with favor You will surround him as with a shield."

---

Writer Henry David Thoreau wrote: "Whate'er we leave to God, God does, and blesses us; the work we choose should be our own, God leaves alone." The first part of this opening line from "Inspiration," one of his many secular poems, always overwhelms me with gratitude.

Today's promise does the same—only more so! Think about it. When we are in "right standing" (AMP) with God, *He*, the holy God of the universe and the eternally righteous One, blesses *us*!

As if that's not enough, in His unmerited favor, He surrounds us with His care and protection.

Blessed promise—blessed Lord!

—BLH

Today's promise:
God *will* bless the righteous.

# JUNE 19

Psalm 91:15, NKJV:
"He shall call upon Me, and I will answer him;
I will be with him in trouble; I will deliver him and honor him."

---

So often we (and by *we*, I mean *I*) read a verse like this and focus on the help that God will give us when we're knee-deep in trials. But isn't it just like God not only to answer us, to be with us in our times of trouble, and to deliver us—but then to *honor* us?

The online *Unabridged Merriam-Webster Dictionary*, in part, defines *honor* as: "to regard or treat with...respect." How amazing is that? God, Who is worthy of *our* deepest honor and praise, says that *He* will honor *us*, respecting when we acknowledge our need of Him by calling on Him and regarding our desire to seek Him as worthy of His blessing.

Now that's a promise with a bonus promise!

—BLH

Today's promise:
God *will* honor *you*!

# JUNE 20

Isaiah 46:4, NASB:
"Even to your old age I will be the same, and even to your graying years I will bear you! I have done it, and I will carry you; and I will bear you and I will deliver you."

---

God is a God of all times and of all seasons of life—from conception in the womb to the gray hairs of old age. God promises to carry us, to bear us, and to save us for our good and His glory. Though we change with age, God and His care remain the same.

In whatever season of life you are, God, Who ages not, will take care of you.

—JGH

Today's promise:
God *will never* change!

# JUNE 21

Psalm 61:3, NKJV:
"For You have been a shelter for me,
a strong tower from the enemy."

---

Before marrying Joe, I lived with and assisted my parents at their home, which was located on a golf course. I recall one day when a particularly windy and clearly dangerous storm appeared quickly, not giving the golfers time to head back to the clubhouse. Seeing several golfers on the green right outside my parents' back door, we invited them in. They were more than grateful to accept and rapidly came into the house, golf clubs and all!

This was a small-scale illustration to me of how God is our shelter when the enemy—whoever or whatever it may be—is quickly approaching. God is there, providing that shelter, that safe haven, that place of rest!

—BLH

Today's promise:
God *is* your shelter!

# JUNE 22

2 Timothy 1:7, AMP:
"For God did not give us a spirit of timidity or cowardice or fear, but [He has given us a spirit] of power and of love and of sound judgment and personal discipline [abilities that result in a calm, well-balanced mind and self-control]."

---

God's gifts to us are always and only good. He gifted them to us with a purpose that included our good and His glory. What He did *not* give us was "a spirit of timidity or cowardice or fear" regarding proclaiming His good news. Those emotions or qualities come directly from the evil one, who places them in our path to keep us from telling others about Christ and His love.

God expects us to utilize His good gift—a spirit "of power and of love and of sound judgment and personal discipline"—when we share the gospel. When these are present, they result in a mind that is "calm, well-balanced," and capable of self-control.

—BLH

Today's promise:
God *will* give you His good gifts for sharing the gospel!

#  JUNE 23

Psalm 16:8, KJV:
"I have set the Lord always before me:
because he is at my right hand, I shall not be moved."

---

I've never done "formation flying"—where two or more airplanes intentionally fly together in close proximity to one another. It is spectacularly demonstrated by the US Air Force's Thunderbirds and the US Navy's Blue Angels—both are outstanding exhibition flying teams! I am told that in formation flying, someone has to be the definitive leader. All other pilots keep their eyes continually fixed on this leader, following his or her lead at all times.

Our truth-promise for today could describe our walk with the Lord in a similar way. By reading His Word, praying to Him, and communing with Him, we stay close to Him. It is there, with Him at our side, that we will remain safe and remain undistracted from where He is leading.

—JGH

Today's promise:
God *will* lead you; follow Him!

# JUNE 24

Psalm 31:23–24, AMP:
"O love the Lord, all you His godly ones!
The Lord preserves the faithful [those with moral and spiritual integrity] and fully repays the [self-righteousness of the] arrogant. Be strong and let your hearts take courage, all you who wait for and confidently expect the Lord."

---

We love the Lord today and for all time not only for Who He is but for what He does (*because* of Who He is). Today's truth-promise states that "the Lord preserves the faithful." He even pays back the proud!

Daniel was placed in a den of lions. But the Lord was with him and brought him through it. The three Hebrew children were placed into the fiery furnace. But the Lord was with them and brought them through it.

We can confidently know that God will be with us and bring us through even the valley of the shadow of death. (See Psalm 23:4.) Therefore, we can take courage, receive God's strength, and hope in God!

—JGH

Today's promise:
God *will* be with you and bring you through your trials!

# JUNE 25

Romans 5:9, AMP:
"Therefore, since we have now been justified [declared free of the guilt of sin] by His blood, [how much more certain is it that] we will be saved from the wrath of God through Him."

---

I would much rather think about the joys of heaven that God has promised to me as His child than I would to dwell on the wrath that He promised that I would be saved from. Yet sometimes it's good for me to remember that if it were not for God's redemptive grace, I would face an eternity apart from Him.

When I am reminded of that truth, it reignites a fire within me to do three things:

- ➤ to recall the mercy and grace of God, without which I would face God's wrath;

- ➤ to be grateful as never before for the fact that I have been "declared free of the guilt of sin"; and

- ➤ to share the gospel with those who do not have that blessed hope and who therefore face the eternal wrath of God.

What a wonderful truth-promise and reminder all in one!

—BLH

Today's promise:
Because of Christ's death, you *are* saved from the wrath of God!

# JUNE 26

1 Peter 3:14–15, AMP:
"But even if you should suffer for the sake of righteousness [though it is not certain that you will], you are still blessed [happy, to be admired and favored by God]. Do not be afraid of their intimidating threats, nor be troubled or disturbed [by their opposition]. But in your hearts set Christ apart [as holy—acknowledging Him, giving Him first place in your lives] as Lord. Always be ready to give a [logical] defense to anyone who asks you to account for the hope and confident assurance [elicited by faith] that is within you, yet [do it] with gentleness and respect."

---

The writer of this truth-promise, Peter, was, in part, teaching believers how to live in an ungodly world. In these verses, he reminded them that they may or may not "suffer for the sake of righteousness." He then encouraged them with the truth that *if* trials came, it didn't mean that God had removed His blessing. On the contrary! They were "still blessed."

Because God's favor on His children was (and is!) secure, they didn't have to spend time being anxious about evil people and their possible threats. Instead, they could focus on giving the Lord first place in their lives. Using their firsthand knowledge of God's grace, they could reply confidently, gently, and respectfully to those who questioned their faith.

—BLH

Today's promise:
God *will* bless you with His favor!

# JUNE 27

Philippians 4:5, AMP:
"Let your gentle spirit [your graciousness, unselfishness, mercy, tolerance, and patience] be known to all people. The Lord is near."

---

What we are and what we do speak louder than what we say. Here I give honor to my dad and praise him for his example.

My dad was unselfish in his provision for our family. He joyfully gave of himself to provide for our needs. He was considerate, and his kindness expressed itself in little ways as he treated my mother with love and devotion. My brother and I always knew that our dad loved our mother.

Dad's forbearing spirit was known at home *and* in the workplace. As a hospital administrator, he dealt with a variety of people and situations. He was so helpful that when he changed jobs, some of the employees would follow him to the new hospital in order to continue to work under his leadership.

When my father was in the final days of his battle with cancer, I gratefully wrote a long letter to him, sharing with him my desire, by God's grace, to be like him.

Today's verse not only gives each of us the reminder to live in such a way that others see Christ in us; it also reminds us of the great truth-promise that we live this way because "the Lord is near!"

—JGH

Today's promise:
God *is* near, enabling you to be an example of grace!

# JUNE 28

Psalm 46:1, KJV:
"God is our refuge and strength, a very present help in trouble."

---

Four years before I was required to retire from my career with the airlines, I had cataract surgery in my left eye. This routine surgery rarely had complications. I anticipated being able to return quickly to flying.

Twenty-four hours after my surgery, I noticed that something was wrong in my eye. My eye doctor quickly examined it and found a very serious retinal tear. He began searching for a retinal specialist to see me as soon as possible. Thankfully, there was one who was available. After evaluating my eye, this specialist told me that I needed an inpatient procedure ASAP.

I quickly prayed to the Lord for help and then agreed to the procedure. It saved my vision and allowed me to finish my flying career.

Today's truth-promise confirmed to me that the Lord truly was present in my time of need. And He remains true to the promise for your needs too!

—JGH

Today's promise:
God *will* be present and will help you in times of trouble!

# JUNE 29

Psalm 139:2–4, NKJV:
"You know my sitting down and my rising up; You understand my thought afar off. You comprehend my path and my lying down, and are acquainted with all my ways. For there is not a word on my tongue, but behold, O Lord, You know it altogether."

---

Just as most newly wedded couples have expressed to us (i.e., "warned" us!), my wife and I now know things about each other that we didn't know prior to our marriage in 2016. After spending so much of our time together since then—after all, we're retired!—we really have come to know each other quite well.

Today's truth-promise says that God knows all about us. God knows us more extensively and deeply than any other person. He knows us mentally, physically, and spiritually. Since God knows us so completely, it is only right for us to agree with the psalmist's prayer at the end of the chapter (see Psalm 139:23–24). We must ask God to search our hearts and thoughts, reveal to us any sin that is there, and lead us in His ways.

—JGH

Today's promise:
God *knows* you!

# JUNE 30

2 Samuel 7:28, NKJV:
"And now, O Lord God, You are God, and Your words are true, and You have promised this goodness to Your servant."

---

In 2 Samuel 7, David was talking about his plans to build the temple. David's prayer of thanksgiving ended the chapter, and today's truth-promise came from that portion of the chapter.

David was specifically praying that God would bless the building of the temple, but the truths he spoke in this verse remain just as true today.

God is true to His Word. He always has been and always will be. That's why when He promised His goodness to David and His blessing on the building of the temple, David knew that he would receive the blessing God had promised to him.

God's Word is filled with the truth God wants to bless you with. Be assured today that He *will* keep His promise to be true to His Word.

—BLH

Today's promise:
God's words are *true*!

# JULY 1

2 Peter 3:9, NASB:
"The Lord is not slow about His promise,
as some count slowness, but is patient toward you,
not wishing for any to perish but for all to come to repentance."

---

As we start the second of the half of the year together, today's great truth-promise is extremely timely. It's a good time for us to be reminded that He knows just the right time, just the right place, and just the right way to fulfill His promises.

We are the ones who need to share His great truth: that He does not wish "for any to perish but for all to come to repentance." We are the ones, however, who are slow—in our obedience.

God is never delayed. He doesn't forget to keep His promises—or worse yet forget that He ever made them. He keeps every promise...every time!

—BLH

Today's promise:
Your promise-keeping God *is* patient.

# JULY 2

Psalm 119:49–50, AMP:
"Remember [always] the word and promise to Your servant, in which You have made me hope. This is my comfort in my affliction, that Your word has revived me and given me life."

---

An old cowboy song, "Home on the Range" has a phrase about the ranchland, telling us that a "discouraging word" is rarely heard there. Discouraging words can weigh us down and give us heavy hearts. Proverbs 12:25 (KJV) starts out this way: "Heaviness in the heart of man maketh it stoop...."

What is the remedy for this? The good Word of God! Proverbs 12:25 (KJV) continues with these words: "But a good word maketh it glad."

Romans 15:4 (AMP) further encourages us: "For whatever was written in earlier times was written for our instruction, so that through endurance and the encouragement of the Scriptures we might have hope and overflow with confidence in His promises."

—JGH

Today's promise:
God's Word *will* revive you and encourage you!

# JULY 3

Luke 6:38, AMP:
"Give, and it will be given to you. They will pour into your lap a good measure—pressed down, shaken together, and running over [with no space left for more]. For with the standard of measurement you use [when you do good to others], it will be measured to you in return."

---

When I read this verse, I usually think of giving financially to the Lord's work. This is something I have tried to do in my life. Being able to give to various ministries that are carrying out the Lord's work, I've received much more in return: a wonderful career that enabled me to give even more generously. Yes, generously—even through salary cutbacks and probable pension termination when the airline went bankrupt.

I think that the principles in this verse can apply to anything that we invest in from a heart of gratitude to God. Supporting His work not only with money but also with time, talents, and service opportunities filled my life with deep, close friendships.

But I must not leave out motivation. We are to give back to God our time, talents, and treasures—not to *get*, but from a heart of gratitude for His gifts to us.

—JGH

Today's promise:
God *will* bless your generous giving.

# JULY 4

1 Corinthians 13:4–8, NKJV:
"Love suffers long and is kind; love does not envy; love does not parade itself, is not puffed up; does not behave rudely, does not seek its own, is not provoked, thinks no evil; does not rejoice in iniquity, but rejoices in the truth; bears all things, believes all things, hopes all things, endures all things. Love never fails...."

---

Love is the great theme of this chapter in the Bible. During premarital counseling, marriage counselors frequently ask couples to put their own names in place of the word *love*. Doing this helps the individuals view love's attributes as intensely personal and practical.

We are not to be overcome by evil but are to overcome evil with good. (See Romans 12:21.) From the verses above, look at the list of evil things that love overcomes:

- impatience
- unkindness
- envy
- boasting
- pride
- rudeness
- selfishness
- anger
- evil thoughts
- iniquity

Love not only overcomes these evils; it also endures, rejoices in the truth, and thinks the best of others. This wonderful attribute can be yours when God's Spirit is in you and controlling you.

—JGH

Today's promise:
Love *never* fails.

# JULY 5

Psalm 145:14, NKJV:
"The Lord upholds all who fall,
and raises up all who are bowed down."

---

Have you ever looked at someone and immediately known that he or she was discouraged? What was it about that individual that portrayed this?

We can usually tell that people are discouraged because of a sad expression on their face or in their eyes; it could have been a slower-than-usual walk or movements; or it could have been, as today's verse says, they are "bowed down"—literally stooped over (even slightly) because of the emotional weight of their burdens.

Today's truth-promise offers hope, encouragement, and help for "*all* who fall" and for "*all* who are bowed down" (emphasis mine). The Lord says, through the psalmist's writing, that He will uphold those who have fallen under the pressures they have encountered. For those whose spirits have weighed them down, He will raise them up.

—BLH

Today's promise:
God *will* raise up those who are bowed down with care.

# JULY 6

Psalm 119:68, NKJV:
"You are good, and do good; teach me Your statutes."

---

God is good. We know this. We see it on a daily basis in the very fact that we have air to breathe, food to eat (in most cases, much more than we need), clothes to wear (and in most cases, to choose from), and a roof over our heads.

But God also *does* good. He provides. He listens. He cares. He guides. He heals. He helps. And so much more!

Our natural response to the fact that these two qualities are both present should be the same as that of the psalmist: "teach me Your statutes." We intuitively want to know more from and about this good Person.

The likely end result of the above? That we will follow His example, obey His teaching, and reflect His goodness.

—BLH

Today's promise:
God *is* good and *does* good!

# JULY 7

Psalm 30:2, ESV:
"O Lord my God, I cried to you for help,
and you have healed me."

---

Healing comes in many forms:

- ➢ healing from addiction
- ➢ healing from the effects of sin
- ➢ healing from illness
- ➢ healing from spiritual separation from God
- ➢ healing from sorrow
- ➢ healing from emotional, spiritual, or physical pain

And it may come here on earth or in eternity. That choice is God's.

We don't know the psalmist's specific need that caused him to cry out to God for help at the outset of today's truth-promise. But we *do* know that he trusted in God to heal him. And God did!

—BLH

Today's promise:
God *will* bring healing—here or in eternity!

# JULY 8

Psalm 144:15, AMP:
"How blessed and favored are the people in such circumstance;
How blessed [fortunate, prosperous, and favored]
are the people whose God is the Lord!"

---

David, the writer of this psalm ("song"), starts this verse by referring to the prosperous scene he had written about in the previous verses: "such circumstances." Those circumstances included:

- ✓ protection from their enemies
- ✓ prosperous families, and
- ✓ plentiful crops.

In listing these blessings, David was reminded (and thereby reminds us) that for those whose God is the Lord, His blessings are abundant—and they are more than enough!

—BLH

Today's promise:
God *blesses* His people!

# JULY 9

Psalm 60:11–12, NKJV:
"Give us help from trouble, for the help of man is useless.
Through God we will do valiantly,
for it is He who shall tread down our enemies."

---

Psalm 60 records King David's thoughts about the various battles he fought with Israel's enemies. He cries to God for help in his time of trouble and declares today's truth-promise: that through God, we will have help when battling our adversaries.

We might not have literal battles to fight, but when confronted by our adversary the devil, we need to claim God's promise that He will help us to achieve the victory.

—JGH

Today's promise:
Through God, you *will* do valiantly!

# JULY 10

Psalm 1:1–2, NASB:
"How blessed is the man who does not walk in the counsel of the wicked, nor stand in the path of sinners, nor sit in the seat of scoffers! But his delight is in the law of the Lord, And in His law he meditates day and night."

---

Two kinds of people are discussed in these verses: the godly and the ungodly. Three life activities are presented: walking, standing, and sitting.

The promised blessing is given to the person who does not follow ungodly advice, live in a sinful way, or reject God's Word.

Blessed people are not perfect. They joyfully use God's Word to regulate all of their life's activities.

—JGH

Today's promise:
God *will* bless you when you walk in His ways!

# JULY 11

Luke 6:22, AMP:
"Blessed [morally courageous and spiritually alive with life-joy in God's goodness] are you when people hate you, and exclude you [from their fellowship], and insult you, and scorn your name as evil because of [your association with] the Son of Man."

---

I know of no one who enjoys being ridiculed, talked about, or "left out." It's not a social status that anyone seeks.

Unfortunately, I *do* know of people who act rudely or crudely and complain loudly and obnoxiously about the customer service while carrying their very large Bibles into the company cafeteria. And it never ceases to amaze me that they say they are seated alone because they are being persecuted for the sake of the gospel. Not so, my friend...not so. You're alone at the table because you're not a nice person!

Today's promise is for those who take a courageous stand to associate themselves with Christ. Their sincerity of heart and the fact that they live with eternity's values in mind gives them a "life-joy in God's goodness." When their focus is firmly fixed on the Author and Finisher of their faith (see Hebrews 12:2), they refuse to take the easy road by condoning sin, even when it means being ridiculed, talked about, or "left out."

And that kind of moral and spiritual courage only exists when God's blessing is present!

—BLH

Today's promise:
God *will* bless those who are treated wrongly for His sake.

# JULY 12

Psalm 51:10, KJV:
"Create in me a clean heart, O God;
and renew a right spirit within me."

---

Okay. So...I messed up. I tried to control what wasn't mine to control. I said what should not have been said. I tried to change what only God can change—if it even needed changing in the first place. And in so doing, I blew it.

But God, in His transforming grace and infinite love, is greater.

Greater than all of my pride.

Greater than my impatience.

Greater than my harsh judgments.

Greater.

I don't know if He will choose to repair what I broke or if He will simply continue to use my brokenness to change me. I only know that He has lovingly, and with the forgiveness He promised, opened my heart to a level of yieldedness I didn't know I needed but that I'm grateful to put into action.

Hands off the control panel. He's got this!

—BLH

Today's promise:
God *will* create a clean heart in you!

# JULY 13

Psalm 23, KJV:
"The Lord is my shepherd; I shall not want.
He maketh me to lie down in green pastures:
he leadeth me beside the still waters. He restoreth my soul:
he leadeth me in the paths of righteousness for his name's sake.
Yea, though I walk through the valley of the shadow of death, I will
fear no evil: for thou art with me; thy rod and thy staff they
comfort me. Thou preparest a table before me in the presence of
mine enemies: thou anointest my head with oil; my cup runneth
over. Surely goodness and mercy shall follow me all the days of my
life: and I will dwell in the house of the Lord for ever."

---

After one of my deepest disappointments, a friend from California said these simple words: "Brenda, where I live, the mountains are beautiful. But the fruit grows in the valleys."

Friend, you may be in the valley, wondering if you'll ever even reach the base of the mountain to start climbing upward again. But look around you.

Ask God to show you the fruit of the Spirit that He is producing in you and through you, right there in your valley.

Use that growth to propel you forward in your walk with Him.

He hasn't forgotten you. He's beside you. With you. Loving you. Caring about your valley moments.

And He's leading you to the place He has chosen for you.

—BLH

Today's promise:
God *will* lead you through the valleys!

# JULY 14

Psalm 28:7, KJV:
"The Lord is my strength and my shield; my heart trusted in him, and I am helped: therefore my heart greatly rejoiceth; and with my song will I praise him."

---

This truth-promise—that God is a strength and shield Who helps us—comes with a proverbial "cherry on top!"

Isn't it awesome that after those times when we need Him to be a shield between us and our problems, to strengthen us, and to help us, God replaces our troubled, fearful heart and gives us a joyful heart?

However, don't confuse joy with mere happiness. Joy runs much deeper and results from a heart that is fully trusting God to strengthen, protect, and help.

In fact, it goes one step further. This joy is so real that it cannot help but flow forth in praise to the Joy-Giver!

—BLH

Today's promise:
God *will* help you and *will* give you joy!

# JULY 15

Joshua 1:9, ESV:
"Have I not commanded you? Be strong and courageous.
Do not be frightened, and do not be dismayed,
for the Lord your God is with you wherever you go."

---

You know that moment when it feels like everything seems to be crashing in around you, and you're just not even certain where to begin to get it all back on track? I had that moment recently. In fact, I began my prayer with these exact three words:

"God, I'm there."

Before I could get out another word, He used this verse to remind me of a worry-silencing truth with these four words:

"I know. I'm here."

—BLH

Today's promise:
God *will* be with you!

# JULY 16

Isaiah 40:8, NASB:
"The grass withers, the flower fades,
but the word of our God stands forever."

---

Yesterday I raked the leaves that had fallen from one of the trees in our front yard. They were late in fading this year, turning from their lush green to shades of yellow and red. But they did eventually fade—and fall.

I'm glad that our God is eternal. He was the same in eternity past as He is in the present and as He will be in eternity future.

We also have God's eternal Word. Scripture is God's "love letter" to us. Its truths will never fade or change. It will stand forever, and God promises that it will accomplish its purpose. (See Isaiah 55:11.)

—JGH

Today's promise:
God's Word *will* stand forever!

# JULY 17

Romans 10:13, KJV:
"For whosoever shall call upon
the name of the Lord shall be saved."

---

All flights have a destination. The pilot wants the navigation—getting from origin to destination—to be certain so that there is no doubt that the final destination will be reached.

Thinking of an airline flight and passengers reminds me that life is full of what I call "be-sure" situations: be sure that the fuel is on board; be sure that the right destination is planned; be sure that this switch is on or that this switch is off; be sure that the flight plan is correct; and the list goes on.

Be-sure navigation (my own terminology) begins with making a good departure—always starting from a known position. That's why believers need a "be-sure" verse. A be-sure Bible verse provides a specific beginning—a definite departure point for walking with God toward an eternal destination.

Today's promise verse (my own "be-sure" verse) assures us that if we have called upon Christ to be our personal Savior, our eternal destination is certain!

—JGH

Today's promise:
When Christ is your Savior, your eternal destination *is* secure!

# JULY 18

Psalm 139:7–10, NKJV:
"Where can I go from Your Spirit? Or where can I flee from Your presence? If I ascend into heaven, You are there; if I make my bed in hell, behold, You are there. If I take the wings of the morning, And dwell in the uttermost parts of the sea, Even there Your hand shall lead me, and Your right hand shall hold me."

---

In this psalm, David tells of the depth of God's knowledge. In these verses, he states that he cannot run from God's presence or from His Spirit. He cannot fly away from God. He cannot swim away from God. David discovers that no one can escape God's presence.

But David discovers another precious thought, declared in today's truth-promise: God's hand leads us, and God's right hand holds us.

—JGH

Today's promise:
Your omnipresent God *will* hold you by the hand.

# JULY 19

Matthew 7:7, KJV:
"Ask, and it shall be given you; seek, and ye shall find; knock, and it shall be opened unto you."

---

I almost avoided including this promise. So often people read this verse when talking about stuff, dreams, or financial prosperity. They make it sound as if they simply need to ask God for any selfish desire, and He'll give it to them.

There's a fine line here, because God *can* give us anything! But He also states in James 4:3 (NASB): "You ask and do not receive, because you ask with wrong motives, so that you may spend it on your pleasures."

However, on the other side of the line, He promises us in today's verse that if we ask, seek, and knock, those things *will* be given, found, and opened.

So perhaps the best answer is for us to test our heart's motives, know the purpose behind our requests, pray that God would answer according to His will, and then ask, seek, and knock with a faith that knows that God can—and will—answer those prayers in the way that is best for us!

—BLH

Today's promise:
God *will* answer your prayer in the way that is best for you!

# JULY 20

Psalm 70:5, ESV:
"But I am poor and needy; hasten to me, O God!
You are my help and my deliverer; O Lord, do not delay!"

---

As David's enemies were quickly approaching, he paused to pray this prayer for help. In this brief verse, he actually leaves for us a clear and concise example of things we should include in our prayers:

- He acknowledged that he needed the Lord.
  - "But I am poor and needy."
- He acknowledged God's specific ability to meet his needs.
  - "You are my help and deliverer."
- He acknowledged his specific needs.
  - "Hasten to me"; "do not delay."

—BLH

Today's promise:
God *is* your help and your deliverer!

## JULY 21

Titus 3:5–6, AMP:
"He saved us, not because of any works of righteousness that we have done, but because of His own compassion and mercy, by the cleansing of the new birth (spiritual transformation, regeneration) and renewing by the Holy Spirit, whom He poured out richly upon us through Jesus Christ our Savior."

---

These verses give a clear description of what God did in our salvation—He gave us delivery from the penalty of sin! Titus uses the word *regeneration*, simply meaning, "born again."

I was born into an earthly family through my physical birth. I was born again into God's family through my spiritual birth.

Did I "work" to get into my physical family? No. Did I have to "work" to get into God's family? No! It was only by God's mercy and grace.

We are saved from the penalty of sin, not through our own work, but through Jesus Christ and His finished work.

—JGH

Today's promise:
Christ *paid* the penalty for your sin!

# JULY 22

Exodus 15:2, NKJV:
"The Lord is my strength and my song, and he has become my salvation; this is my God, and I will praise him,
my father's God, and I will exalt him."

---

When preparing to teach a lesson to a ladies' Sunday school class, I was reading about the life of Moses. Following a train of thought I was formulating in my mind about how to approach the lesson, I decided to read Exodus 2 through Deuteronomy 34 (which covered the lifespan of Moses) and to look for Moses's interactions with God throughout these many chapters in the Bible.

In Exodus chapters 2–14, Moses referred to God by what I would describe as "impersonal" descriptions. But then came chapter 14, where the true story was recorded of how the Israelites walked across the Red Sea on dry ground and how God kept His promise to destroy the Egyptians and the pharaoh who had held them captive in Egypt for so many years. Moses saw firsthand the wonder of his (and our) promise-keeping God.

Today's truth-promise, taken from Exodus 15 (often called the "First Song of Moses") includes some of the first "personalized" comments that Moses made about God. He saw now that God was *his* strength, *his* song, and *his* salvation. Because he now saw God as *his* God, He could not *help* but praise Him.

Neither should we!

—BLH

Today's promise:
God is a *personal* God!

# JULY 23

Ephesians 2:10, NASB:
"For we are His workmanship, created in Christ Jesus
for good works, which God prepared beforehand
so that we would walk in them."

---

I know a master carpenter who does incredible work, and I wondered if he may have been the one who had installed the beautiful molding and fireplace mantels in our home. He told me that the way I would know would be to look for a special cut he makes on the stairway spindles to identify his work.

Today's truth-promise tells us that God, like a master carpenter, works within us to produce good works for Him. Because we are "created in Christ Jesus," we have His mark on us: the life of good works that identifies us as His followers.

—JGH

Today's promise:
You *are* God's workmanship!

## JULY 24

Psalm 107:8, NKJV:
"Oh, that men would give thanks to the Lord for His goodness,
And for His wonderful works to the children of men!"

---

Today's truth-promise is a vivid reminder that God has been, is, and will be good to us.

Oh, that we would take time today to thank Him for that.

—BLH

Today's promise:
God *has been, is, and will be* good to you!

# JULY 25

Psalm 5:11, NKJV:
"But let all those rejoice who put their trust in You;
Let them ever shout for joy, because You defend them;
Let those also who love Your name be joyful in You."

---

"Defense wins championships." I recall hearing that mantra from a record-achieving, award-winning coach, and he had proven it with his well-trained team. His offense heroically scored the goals; his defense courageously prevented the other teams from completing their attempts.

It's probably the football-lover in me taking over, but when I think of defending something or someone, this coach's team comes to mind. Maybe that's why I am so enamored with this word, *defend*, in Scripture. In my mind, it conjures a picture of great strength, perseverance, and fortitude.

And its use in today's truth-promise portrays that perfectly. By defending them, God is providing the strength, perseverance, and fortitude they need.

No wonder they're shouting for joy!

—BLH

Today's promise:
God *is* your defender!

# JULY 26

Psalm 50:15, ESV:
"And call upon me in the day of trouble;
I will deliver you, and you shall glorify me."

———

Deliverance from the Lord may look different each time it shows up. Sometimes the trouble will literally go away—God removes it. Sometimes, the problem or trial will diminish over time, leaving behind a trail of blessing that we cannot see until we reach the end of that particular path in our journey.

And sometimes deliverance comes as we recognize that the problem itself will remain, but that God will be there with us, holding our hand (see Isaiah 41:13) as we walk through it. He may deliver us from the fear that accompanies the problem, empowering us to face it head on. In some cases, He may deliver us by using the words of a friend—or even those of a stranger—to uplift our spirits and encourage us.

But one thing is sure: if God says He will deliver us, He will.

And through the deliverance, we will give Him glory!

—BLH

Today's promise:
He *will* deliver you!

# JULY 27

Proverbs 2:6, NKJV:
"For the Lord gives wisdom;
from His mouth come knowledge and understanding."

---

When I was in college, I thought that I should read up on the classics, such as the writings of the great philosophers Socrates and Plato. May I give you some advice? Don't waste your time!

Yes, their prose certainly is great literature. Yes, they were great thinkers. But they have no godly wisdom. These men fit the description in Scripture of those who never find the truth. (See 2 Timothy 3:7.)

Today's truth-promise gives the Source of truth, wisdom, knowledge, and understanding. It is God, and we receive His truth through His letter to us, His Word.

—JGH

Today's promise:
God *is* the source of all wisdom.

# JULY 28

John 8:36, NKJV:
"Therefore if the Son makes you free,
you shall be free indeed."

---

When Christ makes us free from the bondage of sin, there is no doubt about it. We are "free indeed!"

Yet too often we live like we are bound to sin by chains that can't be broken. We act as if there is no hope.

My friend, today you have hope. Today, the chains of sin cannot and will not bind your heart to the master of all that is evil. Today, you are free—truly free.

The Son of God, Jesus Christ, paid the penalty for your sins and purchased your freedom.

And when Christ pays for your freedom you are indeed—*truly*—free!

—BLH

Today's promise:
When Christ frees you from the power of sin, you are *truly* free!

# JULY 29

Psalm 115:13, AMP:
"He will bless those who fear and worship the Lord
[with awe-inspired reverence and submissive wonder],
both the small and the great."

---

Sometimes we look at the wealthy and think that they have received more of God's blessings, because they have more.

Sometimes we look at those whose business is prospering and think that they have received more of God's blessings, because their company doesn't seem to be struggling in the same way as a smaller business.

Sometimes we look at the large church building and think that they have received more of God's blessings, because they seem to have more people, money, and ministries.

Sometimes we do the opposite, assuming that the smaller of the two in the comparison is more nearly holy or more greatly blessed because they are seemingly not caught up in the distraction of their wealth, importance, or attendance.

Regardless of which approach our thinking took, sometimes we were right, and sometimes we were wrong!

In today's truth-promise, we are reminded that what matters to God is not wealth, importance, or attendance. He will bless those who stand in awe of Him and who reverently worship Him.

—BLH

Today's promise:
God *will* bless your reverent worship of Him!

# JULY 30

1 Corinthians 6:19–20, NKJV:
"Or do you not know that your body is the temple of the Holy Spirit who is in you, whom you have from God, and you are not your own? For you were bought at a price; therefore glorify God in your body and in your spirit, which are God's."

---

In these verses, God tells us that our bodies have a new person living within them as a result of our salvation. The Holy Spirit comes to reside within the believer. This makes us different, special, and valuable.

We are called a "temple," a place where God dwells (and therefore, a place that should be holy). Our bodies are no longer ours, but God's. Therefore, we are to guard our bodies and not defile them with sin.

—JGH

Today's promise:
You *are* the temple where the Holy Spirit dwells.

# JULY 31

Romans 8:35–37, ESV:
"Who shall separate us from the love of Christ? Shall tribulation, or distress, or persecution, or famine, or nakedness, or danger, or sword? As it is written, for your sake we are being killed all the day long; we are regarded as sheep to be slaughtered.
No, in all these things we are more than conquerors through him who loved us."

---

When the author of these verses begins this section by asking a rhetorical question (which usually requires no answer), he takes the time to answer it so that there is no question whatsoever in the reader's mind.

His question asks whether or not any of these things can come between us and the love that Christ has for us, and then he lists some pretty extreme situations—things that would normally sever or at least cripple relationships. However, by his style of writing (i.e., use of the rhetorical question), it seems that the answer of *no* is quite obvious.

However, the answer he provides in verse 37 states a *definitive no* and then offers additional information: These things will not only *not* separate us from Christ's love; we will be "more than conquerors" over these troublesome situations, through the love and strength that Christ provides!

—BLH

Today's promise:
*Nothing* can separate you from Christ's love!

# AUGUST 1

1 Corinthians 10:13, AMP:
"No temptation [regardless of its source] has overtaken or enticed you that is not common to human experience [nor is any temptation unusual or beyond human resistance];
but God is faithful [to His word—He is compassionate and trustworthy], and He will not let you be tempted beyond your ability [to resist], but along with the temptation He [has in the past and is now and] will [always] provide the way out as well, so that you will be able to endure it
[without yielding, and will overcome temptation with joy]."

---

Today's promise verse contains multiple promises and truth-promises. An entire book could be written on this one verse alone. So let's focus on one central truth-promise that makes all the others possible: "God is faithful."

Because of His great faithfulness...

...no temptation is "unusual or beyond human resistance."

...He "is faithful to His Word."

..."He will not let you be tempted beyond your ability [to resist]."

...there is a way out.

..."you will be able to endure it."

..."you will overcome temptation with joy."

"Great is Thy faithfulness!" (See Lamentations 3:23, KJV.)

—BLH

Today's promise:
God *is* faithful!

# AUGUST 2

Romans 8:15–17, NKJV:
"For you did not receive the spirit of bondage again to fear, but you received the Spirit of adoption by whom we cry out, 'Abba, Father.' The Spirit Himself bears witness with our spirit that we are children of God, and if children, then heirs—heirs of God and joint heirs with Christ, if indeed we suffer with Him, that we may also be glorified together."

---

Today's truth-promise sheds light on two glorious and happy benefits that we have as God's children.

First, we have the spirit of adoption, which states that we are now placed into the family of God, with God as our Father. We are not born naturally into His family; we are adopted.

Second, since we are God's children, we have an inheritance. We will receive what God has for us: the glories of heaven for eternity. But the Bible also says that we are equal heirs with Christ, who also gets His inheritance from God.

What a privilege it is to call Him, "Father!"

—JGH

Today's promise:
You, as a believer, are a *child of God*!

# AUGUST 3

Psalm 103:11, KJV:
"For as the heaven is high above the earth,
so great is his mercy toward them that fear him."

———

Today's truth-promise describes the magnitude of God's mercy. This verse calls it "great" mercy. It speaks of its height ("as the heaven is high above the earth").

Three heavens are mentioned in Scripture:

1. The terrestrial heaven is where we live; it's where weather occurs.

2. The celestial heaven is where the stars and planets are.

3. The third heaven is where God dwells.

Astronomers tell us that the universe keeps expanding. Therefore, heaven's height keeps rising. Even so with God's mercy—it continues to grow deeper and higher, with no limits!

—JGH

Today's promise:
God's mercy *is* great!

# AUGUST 4

Psalm 147:4, KJV:
"He counts the number of the stars;
He calls them all by name."

---

This is perhaps one of my favorite truth-promises in the Bible!

For as long as I can remember, I have loved looking at the stars—even as a child. But when I lived in the north woods of Wisconsin for several years, that love increased.

There were no streetlights, no big-city lights, and very little traffic hindering the view of the stars. Their bright lights were a welcome contrast in the darkness and against the black sky. As a result, it literally felt as if I could walk out to my deck, reach up, and grab a star.

Though I am nearly breathless with wonder at the mere memory of those starry nights, I am even more greatly overcome by the fact that my amazing creator God knows exactly how many stars are in His heaven, and He knows each one by its name.

The promise I claim from this truth? He who knows the stars by name (and Who hung them all in space) knows my name too!

Herein is great comfort, joy, and hope!

—BLH

Today's promise:
God, Who knows the stars by name, cares about *you*!

# AUGUST 5

Romans 10:17, AMP:
"So faith comes from hearing [what is told], and what is heard comes by the [preaching of the] message concerning Christ."

---

In Romans 10, Paul is speaking of the fact that people from all backgrounds can avail themselves of the glorious truth of the gospel. In today's truth-promise, he exhorts both listeners and readers of his teaching to preach the message of Christ so that all may come to repentance (see 2 Peter 3:9) and know saving faith.

When we read the Word of God, hear it preached, and take it to heart, it not only produces faith; it then increases our faith. We learn more about our ability to trust God (faith) by reading and hearing His thoughts and words to us.

His Word, producing faith in us, accomplishes God's work through us.

—BLH/JGH

Today's promise:
Faith comes from *hearing and reading* the Word of God.

# AUGUST 6

John 15:5, NASB:
"I am the vine, you are the branches; he who abides in Me and I in him, he bears much fruit, for apart from Me you can do nothing."

---

My sweet husband spoils me, and I don't take it for granted. One of the things he has done many, many times since we were married in 2016 is to bring me fresh flowers. Some of them last for several weeks; others seem to wither, discolor, or start dropping petals in only a matter of days. But they all have one thing in common—once they are cut from their original source, they eventually die, even though I keep in them in clean water and tend to them with careful precision.

In today's truth-promise, Jesus identifies Himself as the Vine.

To help His listeners understand the meaning this name held, He identified them as the branches, explaining to them that they needed the life-giving Vine to survive and to produce fruit in their lives.

Are you bearing spiritual fruit? If not, make sure that you are abiding in the Vine!

—BLH

Today's promise:
When you abide in the Vine, you *will* produce spiritual fruit.

# AUGUST 7

Proverbs 8:32–33, KJV:
"Now therefore hearken unto me, O ye children: for blessed are they that keep my ways. Hear instruction, and be wise, and refuse it not."

---

When I was in the seventh grade, our teacher gave us one of those fake tests. When she handed out the test, she was very clear that we were to read the directions before starting the timed test! The directions, printed at the top of the page, stated something like: "Do not begin this test with the first question. Instead, turn the paper over, read the final question, and follow the directions given there."

The final question said, "If you answered this question first, please put an 'A+' at the top of the front page and wait quietly for your disobedient classmates to finish all the other questions!"

Wisdom is actually the speaker in today's truth-promise. She (as Scripture refers to her) promises that those who listen to her and act on her teaching will be blessed. She is, as her name implies, a wise teacher, because she repeats her instructions in a more concise way and then reminds us, her students, not to refuse her teaching!

—BLH

Today's promise:
God *will* bless you for walking in wisdom.

# AUGUST 8

Psalm 27:1, KJV:
"The Lord is my light and my salvation; whom shall I fear?
the Lord is the strength of my life; of whom shall I be afraid?"

---

David, the author of this psalm, knew that we need light, salvation, and strength.

We need light—not just to see our way, but spiritual light, which we get from God's Word. (See Psalm 119:130.) When we receive light (both physical and spiritual), we do not need to fear the dark (again, both physically and spiritually).

We need salvation—the forgiveness of sins, with the destiny of heaven. When we accept God's gift of salvation, we no longer need to fear eternity.

We need strength, because we get weary. David tells us in this truth-promise that God is our strength.

When God is our light, salvation, and strength, we have no cause to fear, because His perfect love casts out fear. (See 1 John 4:18.)

—JGH

Today's promise:
God *is* your light, salvation, and strength.

# AUGUST 9

John 20:29, ESV:
"Jesus said to him, 'Have you believed because you have seen me? Blessed are those who have not seen and yet have believed.'"

---

Poor Thomas. The man Jesus is speaking to in this truth-promise verse will forever be known as "Doubting Thomas." Though he knew Jesus with a firsthand knowledge, he did not believe that Christ truly had risen from the dead until he saw the scars in Jesus's hands.

Throughout the promises in this book, we've seen Jesus blessing and honoring our faith and trust in Him. This verse is no different. Jesus tells Thomas—and us—that those who believe in the unseen God are "spiritually secure" (AMP) and have God's blessing!

"Though you have not seen him, you love him. Though you do not now see him, you believe in him and rejoice with joy that is inexpressible and filled with glory" (1 Peter 1:8. ESV).

—BLH

Today's promise:
God *will* bless your faith!

# AUGUST 10

Matthew 5:4, KJV:
"Blessed are they that mourn: for they shall be comforted."

---

In 2015 my family and I had two funerals in one month—one for my late wife and one for my aunt. Since they were very close together in time, we had to decide which family members would attend which funeral, because the distance and timing prohibited everyone from attending *both* funerals. Brenda's dad had also passed away earlier the same year.

Where did we find comfort in our times of earthly sorrow? We had the promises of God and His Word, and we experienced the patience and comfort of the Scriptures, as seen in Romans 15:4.

Nothing else could have provided the level of comfort we found in His Word. God's Word told us where our loved ones were—in heaven with Him—because of their faith in Christ. In our time of mourning, this was a great comfort.

—JGH

Today's promise:
God *will* comfort those who mourn.

# AUGUST 11

Psalm 31:19, KJV:
"Oh how great is thy goodness, which thou hast laid up for them that fear thee; which thou hast wrought for them that trust in thee before the sons of men!"

---

The fear of God in this truth-promise verse refers to an awe for Who He is, not the "scary" kind of fear. In fact, when you stand in awe of Him and look at both His mighty acts and His tender love on your behalf, you cannot help but see His goodness all around you.

—BLH

Today's promise:
God's goodness is *great*!

# AUGUST 12

Proverbs 8:17, KJV:
"I love them that love me;
and those that seek me early shall find me."

---

Today's truth-promise personally warms my heart. It is from the book of Proverbs, which I began reading early in my Christian life. By reading a chapter a day in a thirty-one-day month, I could read the entire book in one month.

Proverbs is not only a book of spiritual wisdom; it is a book of practical wisdom, dealing with many topics. It provided tremendous help for me when dealing with various people and situations while working for the airlines. It helped with family and parenting issues, money and work issues, and the list goes on.

I fell in love with Proverbs and its wisdom. Our truth-promise really is true: Wisdom will return your affectionate interest.

—JGH

Today's promise:
You *will* find wisdom in God's Word.

# AUGUST 13

1 John 1:9, KJV:
"If we confess our sins, he is faithful and just
to forgive us our sins, and to cleanse us
from all unrighteousness."

---

God gave me Christian parents who loved God, loved each other, and loved me. This love included discipline and correction when I did wrong—which was often! Bringing home a bad grade on my "Behavior Report" declared my lack of self-control and my love for talking—both besetting sins.

My dad would frown at the grade, express his disappointment, and tell me that I could—and should—do better. With a sincere and sorrowful confession, I received forgiveness every time.

When we confess our sins, our wonderful heavenly Father faithfully extends forgiveness and complete cleansing from unrighteousness.

—JGH

Today's promise:
When you confess your sins, God *will* forgive them!

# AUGUST 14

Psalm 128:1–4, NKJV:
"Blessed is every one who fears the Lord, who walks in His ways.
When you eat the labor of your hands,
you shall be happy, and it shall be well with you. Your wife shall
be like a fruitful vine in the very heart of your house,
your children like olive plants all around your table.
Behold, thus shall the man be blessed who fears the Lord."

―――

Two of the natural byproducts of a life lived for God are the privilege of receiving His blessings and the joy of experiencing them.

Seeing God for Who He is (and thereby standing in reverent awe of Him) impacts every area of your life:

> ➤ Your direction (walk "in His ways")

> ➤ Your diligence (eat "the labor of your hands")

> ➤ Your delights (enjoy your loved ones)

> ➤ Your destiny (know God's blessing)

—BLH

Today's promise:
When you fear the Lord, God *will* bless you!

# AUGUST 15

Isaiah 43:1, AMP:
"But now, this is what the Lord, your Creator says, O Jacob,
and He who formed you, O Israel,
'Do not fear, for I have redeemed you [from captivity];
I have called you by name; you are Mine!'"

---

In today's verse, God is speaking directly to the nation of Israel. He wraps His arms around them and reminds them that because they belong to Him, He has redeemed them from their captivity in Egypt and has claimed them as His own. That's quite a gift.

But in many ways these truth-promises are ours as well, because God spoke very similar words to us through His Word:

He redeems us!
"In whom we have redemption through his blood, the forgiveness of sins, according to the riches of his grace" (Ephesians 1:7, KJV).

He calls us by name!
"But he that entereth in by the door is the shepherd of the sheep. To him the porter openeth; and the sheep hear his voice: and he calleth his own sheep by name, and leadeth them out" (John 10:2–3, KJV).

We belong to Him!
"Behold what manner of love the Father has bestowed on us, that we should be called children of God" (1 John 3:1, NKJV).

—BLH

Today's promise:
God *knows* your name!

# AUGUST 16

Psalm 31:7, AMP:
"I will rejoice and be glad in Your steadfast love,
because You have seen my affliction;
You have taken note of my life's distresses."

---

Many of the psalms of David were written out of his response to the fact that enemies sought to destroy him. His psalms include songs in which he pled for God's help, songs in which he poured out his heart before the Lord, and songs of praise (like the one from which today's truth-promise was taken).

God was fully aware of David's situations. He knew all about the problems David had encountered and the afflictions he had faced. David acknowledges this and expresses his praise to God because of it.

When you're going through whatever that season's struggle may be, it's hard to see where you are headed. But David's God—*your* God—has taken note of it, and His mercy and grace will guide you through it!

—BLH

Today's promise:
God *is* aware of what is happening in your life!

# AUGUST 17

Matthew 5:9, KJV:
"Blessed are the peacemakers:
for they shall be called the children of God."

---

In some of the Bible-preaching churches I've attended, there has been division and strife. This has always been a sad situation to me.

In 1 Thessalonians 5:13–14 (KJV), Paul appeals to the church members there to "be at peace" among themselves. In the context of this appeal, the apostle asks (verse 13) that they give esteem to the pastoral leadership and warn the unruly; he further admonishes the members to "have patience with all men" (verse 14).

I've known pastors who were called of God to step in and lead these churches that were laden with strife and division. Through God's gentle leading, these men were able to "pour oil on the waters."

These peacemaker pastors are God's blessing to His people and can be called children of God, after our Savior, Who is the Prince of Peace.

—JGH

Today's promise:
God *will* bless the peacemakers among His children.

# AUGUST 18

Psalm 119:32, AMP:
"I will run the way of Your commandments [with purpose],
For You will give me a heart that is willing."

---

I'm a problem-solver by nature. One of my strengths is my ability to identify a problem and then find a solution for it. But I have sat through countless meetings in my lifetime in which ninety-five percent of the time is spent on identifying the problem and then rehashing its history and recalling all the difficulties that have come because of the problem. I sit there, thinking: *Aaargh—we've identified the problem; let's get a solution started!*

God created us, so He knows us better than anyone. He knows that we are all too often like the problem-*finding* committee members, dwelling on our problems and all the difficulties related to them.

In today's promise verse, the psalmist wisely acknowledges that between the problem (sin) and the solution (following God's commands), a bridge is necessary: the willingness to implement the change!

When God gives you the willingness to make those necessary changes, run with purpose toward that goal!

—BLH

Today's promise:
God *will* give you a willing heart!

# AUGUST 19

Psalm 59:17, ESV:
"O my Strength, I will sing praises to you,
for you, O God, are my fortress,
the God who shows me steadfast love."

---

We have a favorite getaway spot less than two hours from our home. It's not extravagantly elegant or even elaborately decorated. It's just this beautifully cozy spot with a gracious atmosphere, the best breakfasts on the planet, and an attention to detail like no other establishment I know of. We always walk into our favorite cottage room and comment: "It's the little things...."

That's the expression that came to mind when I saw today's truth-promise: "It's the little things." No, the description of God is not by any means little, with words like: *strength*, *fortress*, and *steadfast*.

However, the psalmist uses a wonderful "little" verb that has probably slipped by me many times in the past—but not today; it's the word *shows*. He describes the Lord as: "the God who *shows* me steadfast love" (emphasis mine).

God not only has these qualities; He *shows* them to us—demonstrates them by His actions; allows us to be the recipients of them!

And that's not such a little thing after all!

—BLH

Today's promise:
God *shows* you His steadfast love!

# AUGUST 20

Deuteronomy 7:9, KJV:
"Know therefore that the Lord thy God, he is God, the faithful God, which keepeth covenant and mercy with them that love him and keep his commandments to a thousand generations."

---

One of the traits I most appreciate in friends and coworkers is loyalty. I've got their backs, so I want to know—without a doubt—that they've got mine!

In this verse, Moses is telling the Israelites that God is loyal, not only to them (His chosen people) but also to His covenant (His abiding promises to them). Those attributes of God have not changed and are truth-promises that we can hold on to and expect God to honor even today.

After all, "He is God, the faithful God."

—BLH

Today's promise:
God *is* the faithful God!

# AUGUST 21

Proverbs 2:7, AMP:
"He stores away sound wisdom for the righteous [those who are in right standing with Him]; He is a shield to those who walk in integrity [those of honorable character and moral courage]."

---

I've been blessed with some pretty amazing, skilled, and gifted teachers in my lifetime. Many were well-known specialists in their fields of expertise—considered the best of the best, in some cases—and I am more grateful than I could ever fully express.

In today's truth-promise, the All-Wise God, Who not only has all wisdom but is in His very nature wisdom itself, has stored away "sound wisdom" for "those who are in right standing with Him." Talk about receiving instruction from the Best of the Best! What an honor! And what a responsibility!

Perhaps that's why, in the conclusion of the verse, He promises us with the truth that He will be a shield for us as we strive to put this wisdom into practice by living lives of integrity.

—BLH

Today's promise:
God *will* give you wisdom!

# AUGUST 22

1 John 4:7–8, AMP:
"Beloved, let us [unselfishly] love and seek the best for one another, for love is from God; and everyone who loves [others] is born of God and knows God [through personal experience]. The one who does not love has not become acquainted with God [does not and never did know Him], for God is love. [He is the originator of love, and it is an enduring attribute of His nature.]"

---

It's interesting to see family resemblances between children and parents. These similarities may be physical, mental, or seen in personality likenesses.

Therefore, as children of God, we should carry a family resemblance—especially the Father's attribute of love. Jesus says that others will know that we are His if we love one another. (See John 13:35.)

When considering this truth-promise today, ask God to strengthen your love for others so that you may be more like Him.

—JGH

Today's promise:
God *is* love!

# AUGUST 23

Psalm 118:1, NKJV:
"Oh, give thanks to the Lord, for He is good!
For His mercy endures forever."

---

Several years ago, a friend of mine was telling me about the man she was dating. I was pleased that she *started* with a description of the godly fruits she saw lived out in his life and *then* described how "super cute" she thought he was! She ended with, "He's a *good* man, Brenda."

That simple closing description said so much. It told me that he was consistent in who he was. It told me that he was known by others for being a good man. It told me that he was trustworthy.

Today's truth-promise describes our merciful God that way as well. The meaning is very much the same as the one implied by my friend—only God's goodness is on a much larger scale, in every possible way: our God is consistent in Who He is; He is known for His goodness; He is trustworthy.

(And just so you know...my friend and her good man? They are married and have four children!)

—BLH

Today's promise:
God is *good*!

# AUGUST 24

Psalm 103:8, NKJV:
"The Lord is merciful and gracious,
Slow to anger, and abounding in mercy."

---

The "Patty Positive" in me looks at a verse like today's truth-promise and sees the "happy" words: *merciful, gracious, abounding*! I see the word *anger*, and I tend to want to skip over it and move on to the happy words!

But stop and look at the description (and therefore, truth-promise) about Who our God is: He is a God Who is *slow* to anger.

Because of our propensity to sin oh so easily, imagine if He *weren't* "slow to anger." We would only ever know His wrath and never get to experience the fact that He is "merciful and gracious...and abounding in mercy!"

—BLH

Today's promise:
God *is* slow to anger!

# AUGUST 25

Isaiah 54:10, NKJV:
"'For the mountains shall depart and the hills be removed, but My kindness shall not depart from you, nor shall My covenant of peace be removed,' says the Lord, who has mercy on you."

---

Today's promise is another of those that was first given by God to the children of Israel. In His infinite love, He was assuring them that He would not turn His back on them.

Once again, we know that our great God is the God of the children of Israel, but He is our God as well. His promises to them often mirror promises to us or include promises that are still ours to claim and hold on to today, thousands of years later.

God's promise in this verse that His kindness will not depart and that He has mercy on us certainly applies to all of us. Romans 8:38–39 reminds us that nothing at all can separate us from His love, so I'm sure that includes departing mountains and no-longer-existent hills!

—BLH

Today's promise:
God *is* kind and merciful!

# AUGUST 26

Psalm 86:5, ESV:
"For you, O Lord, are good and forgiving,
abounding in steadfast love to all who call upon you."

---

It is to my shame that I confess my quickness to "write someone off" once that individual has "done me wrong." It is only when I remember God's steadfast love—His mercy in withholding from me what I truly deserve—that I can see my way through to the necessary heart of forgiveness.

This is one of those verses that is a promise, not in word, but in its foundation on the character of God. Because of Who He is—good, forgiving, abounding in mercy—He will forgive me when I call on Him.

Precious, precious promise.

—BLH

Today's promise:
God *will* extend mercy when I call on Him!

# AUGUST 27

Psalm 147:3, KJV:
"He heals the brokenhearted
And binds up their wounds."

---

Joseph, rejected by his brothers and sold into slavery, had plenty to break his heart and wound his spirit. But I love the fact that when naming his sons (see Genesis 41:51), he gave eloquent testimony regarding the God of broken hearts and wounded spirits.

His first son was named Manasseh, which meant *forgetting*. Joseph's choice of this name said to all that God had helped him to forget his toil and trouble.

Joseph's next son was named Ephraim. His name meant *fruitful*. In choosing this name, Joseph said that God had given him success "in the land of his affliction."

Perhaps this change in his heart and the healing God gave to his spirit allowed Joseph to declare, when reunited with his brothers, "Ye thought evil against me; but God meant it unto good" (Genesis 50:20, KJV).

—JGH

Today's promise:
God *will* heal the brokenhearted.

# AUGUST 28

Psalm 121:2, NKJV:
"My help comes from the Lord, Who made heaven and earth."

---

There is a beautiful elegance in simplicity. This is true of art, decorating, clothing, and today's truth-promise.

God, Who made heaven and earth...

> ...(let the magnitude of what He did in the act of creation sink in here)...

...is the Source of your help.

What an empowering truth!

—BLH

Today's promise:
Your help comes from the creator of *all* things!

# AUGUST 29

Exodus 20:12, AMP:
"Honor (respect, obey, care for) your father and your mother, so that your days may be prolonged in the land the Lord your God gives you."

---

This commandment is repeated in the New Testament in Ephesians 6:2. Both references stress rendering to parents honor, respect, and courtesy, with the promise of longevity of life. It is a joyous and appropriate thing to see children obeying the Lord in observing this commandment.

On the other hand, it is sad to see parents mocked, mistreated, and dishonored. In fact, a warning is given against this in Proverbs 30:17.

Even if your parents are not deserving of honor, you should honor them, because God commands it, it is Christlike, and He will give you grace to do your part.

—JGH

Today's promise:
God *will* bless you for honoring your parents!

# AUGUST 30

Psalm 48:14, KJV:
"For this God is our God for ever and ever:
he will be our guide even unto death."

———

The gifts and strengths God entrusted to my dad allowed him to serve vocationally in several churches during his years in the pastorate. We lived in various states over the course of those years.

Perhaps that's why I always envied my friends who had grown up in the same town where they were born and who later returned to that town to retain it as *their* hometown. I always longed for a constant: a lifelong friend, a home that held years and years of our family's memories, or just the certainty that I wouldn't have to be the new kid once again. God had different—and better, as I now know—plans for me.

I was well into my adult years when I finally realized the truth that is found in today's promise: the Lord was going to be my God and my guide all throughout my life. The security that came from that knowledge was far greater than any home, earthly friendship, or geographical hometown ever could have provided. God was—and remains—my "constant."

—BLH

Today's promise:
God *will* be your guide!

# AUGUST 31

Ephesians 2:8, NASB:
"For by grace you have been saved through faith;
and that not of yourselves, it is the gift of God."

---

As I looked at this very familiar, oft-quoted truth-promise, there were so many things that came to mind. Then I read it in the Amplified Bible, and it spoke the truth so beautifully, that I decided to let it do the thought-sharing today:

"For it is by grace [God's remarkable compassion and favor drawing you to Christ] that you have been saved [actually delivered from judgment and given eternal life] through faith. And this [salvation] is not of yourselves [not through your own effort], but it is the [undeserved, gracious] gift of God."

—BLH

Today's promise:
Salvation is God gracious *gift* to you!

# SEPTEMBER 1

2 Peter 1:3–4, NKJV:
"As His divine power has given to us all things that pertain to life and godliness, through the knowledge of Him who called us by glory and virtue, by which have been given to us exceedingly great and precious promises, that through these you may be partakers of the divine nature, having escaped the corruption that is in the world through lust."

---

Every airliner I flew had a flight manual. It was a big, thick, ring-bound volume that had all the information we needed to operate the airplane. Pilots studied it, restudied it, and carried it for ready reference while in flight.

God has given us His manual for "life and godliness." It is the Bible, His written Word. In God's Word, we have everything we need to know to live for Him.

—JGH

Today's promise:
God *will* use His Word to teach you!

# SEPTEMBER 2

Proverbs 4:10, KJV:
"Hear, O my son, and receive my sayings;
and the years of thy life shall be many."

---

When He gave the Ten Commandments to Moses, God added a promise to one of them: He promised long life to those who would honor their parents. (See Exodus 20:12.) Paul reminds the believers in Ephesus of this command and promise as well. (See Ephesians 6:2–3.)

In today's truth-promise from Proverbs, the writer told his son to listen to what he was teaching him. This wise father had walked many paths through the years—some of them the right path; others were clearly a wrong path—and he had acquired a great deal of experience (and the wisdom he had gleaned from it) to pass along.

Listening to godly advice from those who are older than we are will always be time well spent. Following their godly teaching will certainly bring blessings and spiritual benefits.

—BLH

Today's promise:
God *will* honor your respect for godly wisdom.

# SEPTEMBER 3

Psalm 118:23, KJV:
"This is the Lord's doing; it is marvelous in our eyes."

---

Today is our wedding anniversary! In a very brief summary, we will simply share that Joe's first wife—who was my father's secretary many years ago and who was a dear friend of mine—passed away in 2015 after an extended battle with heart disease.

I had never married, and as Joe began praying for a helpmeet, God directed him to pursue the possibility of changing this old family friendship into a dating relationship. At first, I think we were both as shocked as the other, seeing what God was doing.

But that was exactly what was happening—*God* was doing it. He was bringing beauty out of the ashes of earthly loss (see Isaiah 61:3). Early in our relationship we claimed today's verse as "ours." We included it on the favors we gave to our wedding guests and have it on pictures and plaques throughout our home. Mostly, we cherish it in our hearts.

We share this story today not to be all mushy and gushy but to remind you of this truth-promise straight out of God's Word—that when God does it, it's marvelous!

—BLH/JGH

Today's promise:
When God does it, it's *marvelous!*

# SEPTEMBER 4

John 9:1–3, ESV:
"As he passed by, he saw a man blind from birth.
And his disciples asked him, 'Rabbi, who sinned, this man or his parents, that he was born blind?'
Jesus answered, 'It was not that this man sinned, or his parents, but that the works of God might be displayed in him.'"

———

Something inside us—pride? control (an offshoot of pride)? a desire to find the answer so that we can find the solution (again, often a byproduct of pride)? a hope that we can prevent it from happening again, or to others, or to us (yup, also related to pride)?—needs to know why bad things happen. No, the motives aren't always foundationally bad, but the answers aren't always available in this lifetime on earth either.

Sometimes we have only one answer: "This happened 'that the works of God might be displayed in him.'"

And in the end, that is enough.

—BLH

Today's promise:
God *will* display His works through what He entrusts to you!

# SEPTEMBER 5

Romans 5:8, NASB:
"But God demonstrates His own love toward us,
in that while we were yet sinners, Christ died for us."

---

Not long ago, the power, scope, magnitude, and truth of this verse grabbed my thoughts and wouldn't let go. With tears streaming down my cheeks, I thanked God for this amazing gift in a deeper way than I had ever thanked Him before.

There was Christ, the sinless Lamb of God, looking at what He was about to do—die for something He didn't do, for people who didn't love Him, to save them from something they deserved and He didn't.

And He did it anyway, because it was why He had come to earth. It was His purpose, His mission, His gift.

Herein is love.

—BLH

Today's promise:
Christ died for *you*!

## SEPTEMBER 6

2 Corinthians 12:9, AMP:
"But He has said to me, 'My grace is sufficient for you [My lovingkindness and My mercy are more than enough—always available—regardless of the situation]; for [My] power is being perfected [and is completed and shows itself most effectively] in [your] weakness.' Therefore, I will all the more gladly boast in my weaknesses, so that the power of Christ [may completely enfold me and] may dwell in me."

―――――

The next time you feel inadequate or incapable of accomplishing the task, project, or ministry opportunity that has been entrusted to you, grab this verse and claim its truth-promises!

When you feel weak (insufficient for the task), it's a great thing! It means that there's room to see God's power at work! It means that His grace will not only show up, but it will shine through!

—BLH

Today's promise:
God's power and grace *will* be greater than your weakness!

# SEPTEMBER 7

Isaiah 12:3, KJV:
"Therefore with joy shall ye draw water
out of the wells of salvation."

---

Happiness is the illusive state all humankind seeks. Some seek their happiness in wealth. Some seek their happiness in position. Some seek their happiness in things.

For the believer, joy is so much more than happiness. Joy, which has its roots in our salvation, comes from a well that will never run dry and is therefore not dependent on outward circumstances. True joy is found in Christ alone!

—BLH/JGH

Today's promise:
Salvation in Christ brings *true* joy!

# SEPTEMBER 8

Colossians 2:10, AMP:
"And in Him you have been made complete [achieving spiritual stature through Christ], and He is the head over all rule and authority [of every angelic and earthly power]."

---

When Christ died on the cross, He cried out, "It is finished." (See John 19:30.) The work He had come to do was complete. Nothing further was needed.

In today's glorious truth-promise, He assures us that because of Christ's death, we, as believers, are complete in Him. We need to do nothing further. We need to say nothing further. We need nothing further.

Finished. Done. Complete!

—BLH

Today's promise:
You are *complete* in Christ!

# SEPTEMBER 9

Psalm 108:12–13, NKJV:
"Give us help from trouble, for the help of man is useless.
Through God we will do valiantly,
for it is He who shall tread down our enemies."

---

We will all have trouble at some point in this life. (See Job 5:7.) To whom are we to turn when those troubles come?

The psalmist observes that if we seek only *human* wisdom and counsel in times of trouble, it will be worthless. However, in asking for God's help in these times, He may lead us to *godly* wisdom and counsel that He will use to give us the victory over the trials we are facing.

—JGH

Today's promise:
God *will* use wise counsel to lead you to victory over trials!

# SEPTEMBER 10

Colossians 1:13–14, NASB:
"For He rescued us from the domain of darkness, and transferred us to the kingdom of His beloved Son, in whom we have redemption, the forgiveness of sins."

Let today's truth-promise remind you and assure you of three specific things that God has done on your behalf and because of His great love:

- He rescued you—"from the domain of darkness."

- He relocated you—"to the kingdom of His beloved Son."

- He redeemed you—gave you "the forgiveness of sins!"

—BLH

Today's promise:
You have been *redeemed*!

# SEPTEMBER 11

Hebrews 13:6, AMP:
"So we take comfort and are encouraged and confidently say, 'The Lord is my Helper [in time of need], I will not be afraid. What will man do to me?'"

---

On September 11, 2001, my brother, as part of his normal morning schedule, was at the World Trade Center. I won't rehash the events of this sad and all-too-familiar day, but I will quickly state that my brother had already left the WTC prior to the horrific attack on these buildings—and on our country. However, I did not know for almost three hours that he was not one of those buried in the rubble.

My emotions ran the entire gamut that day. I so greatly longed to follow the advice that many were tossing out like free candy in a parade: "Just trust in God." Although that was my heart's desire, I found the reality of fear a little less easy to toss aside than I had hoped it would be.

A dear friend shared today's truth-promise with me that evening, and its words penetrated deeply into my soul. The events of the day had left me with a sense of fear. Yet I did not need to fear what evil people were trying to do to our nation. God would help me in my time of need. (Note that He did not promise to protect me from *having* a time of need.)

I took great comfort—and even encouragement—from that truth, allowing me to confidently say, "I will not be afraid."

Take comfort, friend. The Lord is your helper!

—BLH

Today's promise:
The Lord *will* be your helper!

# SEPTEMBER 12

Psalm 116:6–8, NKJV:
"The Lord preserves the simple; I was brought low,
and He saved me. Return to your rest, O my soul,
for the Lord has dealt bountifully with you.
For You have delivered my soul from death,
my eyes from tears, and my feet from falling."

---

God's help and deliverance are comprehensive and all-inclusive. Some of His gracious and merciful help is provided for our time on earth. Some of His help is for eternity.

For example, removing our tears could be temporal (for a time) or for eternity. Our deliverance from spiritual death (salvation) is for eternity.

Keeping our "feet from falling" speaks of His guiding our daily steps away from the pitfalls of this life.

All of these, whether temporal or eternal, are His bountiful dealings with us!

—JGH

Today's promise:
God *will* deal bountifully with His children!

# SEPTEMBER 13

Jeremiah 18:4, AMP:
"But the vessel that he was making from clay was spoiled by the potter's hand; so he made it over, reworking it and making it into another pot that seemed good to him."

---

Jeremiah witnessed the potter's actions, and God used that scene to teach Jeremiah (and thereby us) a great truth-promise: "So He made it over."

We are not disposable to God! He has placed a value on us (through the blood of Christ) that will never diminish! So when we are "marred," He chooses to remake us—perhaps for a different use or purpose or with an updated design or function, but He doesn't dispose of us!

Oh the blessed intermingling of grace and hope!

—BLH

Today's promise:
God *will* make you over!

# SEPTEMBER 14

Luke 5:12, NASB:
"While He was in one of the cities, behold, there was a man covered with leprosy; and when he saw Jesus, he fell on his face and implored Him, saying,
'Lord, if You are willing, You can make me clean.'"

---

My precious friend Amy calls it carpet-smelling prayer. I think the motivation behind a prayer with this much emotion, this much passion, this much desire comes from the action described in the four words that precede his falling on his face before the Lord: "when he saw Jesus."

Oh sure, we read about Jesus. We talk about Jesus. We even sing about Jesus. But when was the last time we saw Jesus? No I'm not being mystical or speaking of physically viewing the living, breathing Son of God sitting across the room. I'm speaking of a much deeper view: a view that transcends mere vision.

For example, when I truly see Him for who He is and think of the Lord as my shepherd, I don't merely envision a male human being tending bleating sheep. I don't even simply picture the Lord Himself walking with me, staff in one hand, my hand in the other, as I find rest beside still waters—as awesome as that thought is. When I know Him and have a firsthand understanding of the depth of His character, I see in that title "shepherd" the overwhelming truth that because of who He is, "I shall not want." It encompasses the entirety of His being, His power, and His love.

Today's truth-promise reminds us to know Him, to fall on our faces before, and to know that He longs to make us clean!

—BLH

Today's promise:
God *will* make you clean!

# SEPTEMBER 15

John 15:12, KJV:
"This is my commandment,
That ye love one another, as I have loved you"

---

People are hard to love sometimes—even other believers. Yet our Lord simply commands us to love each other, *as* He loved us:

- ❖ without conditions
- ❖ without restrictions
- ❖ without agendas

Christ loved us when we were unlovely.

Is there anyone you find hard to love? Then go, be Christ to that person!

—JGH

Today's promise:
Christ loves you *unconditionally*!

# SEPTEMBER 16

Matthew 11:29, NASB:
"Take My yoke upon you and learn from Me, for I am gentle and humble in heart, and you will find rest for your souls."

---

My mind races with thoughts, ides, what-ifs, and coulda-shoulda-wouldas too many hours on too many days. Truth be told, I waste more time than I care to admit fretting and stewing and creating imaginary conversations in an attempt to fix nonexistent problems!

Yet, here is Christ, in gentle and unhurried tones, inviting me to learn from Him. He reminds me, through softly spoken words, that He is gentle, that His heart is humble.

And then, then comes that comforting promise. You know the kind I mean: the kind where the sigh of letting go of the turmoil in my spirit is almost audible. The kind of promise that is so genuine it brings rest to my stirred-up soul.

I learn of Him—through His Word.

I am comforted by the knowledge of His gentleness and humility.

I find rest. His rest. And my soul is at peace.

—BLH

Today's promise:
God *will* give you rest for your soul.

# SEPTEMBER 17

Psalm 147:11, AMP:
"The Lord favors those who fear and worship Him [with awe-inspired reverence and obedience],
Those who wait for His mercy and lovingkindness."

---

During my years as a music teacher in various Christian and private schools, it made perfect sense to me that I was not to have "favorites." But I'll let you in on a little secret: teachers do have students who, while not favorites, are a little extra special! I would more likely gravitate toward respectful, trustworthy, hard-working students for special, honored tasks than students who were rude, lazy, or could not be trusted.

While the Bible *does* tell us in Acts 10:34 and Romans 2:11 that God does not show partiality when it comes to His free gift of salvation, today's truth-promise clearly states that He "favors those who fear and worship Him."

The favor He shows is the blessing that comes to those who revere His holiness, sincerely worship Him, and patiently wait for His mercy.

—BLH

Today's promise:
God *will* show favor on you for trusting in Him!

# SEPTEMBER 18

John 14:16–17, NKJV:
"And I will pray the Father, and He will give you another Helper, that He may abide with you forever—the Spirit of truth, whom the world cannot receive, because it neither sees Him nor knows Him; but you know Him, for He dwells with you and will be in you."

---

People who "come alongside" to be with us, to help us, and to strengthen us are a great comfort to us. This very word, *comfort*, describes today's promise.

Our Lord says that He will ask God the Father to send us such a One (to be with us forever) in the Person of the Holy Spirit. Counselor, Helper, Intercessor, and Advocate are not only some of the names by which He is called. They are also words that beautifully describe His promised help to us.

—JGH

Today's promise:
The Holy Spirit *will* dwell in you and help you!

# SEPTEMBER 19

Isaiah 53:6, KJV:
"All we like sheep have gone astray; we have turned every one to his own way; and the Lord hath laid on him the iniquity of us all."

---

I was the one who had sinned. I was the one who had gone my own way.

But today's truth-promise gives us the glorious undeserved gift that is promised to us from our loving God: He laid our sin—our horrid, smelly, evil sins on His sinless, spotless Son.

Promise fulfilled!

—BLH

Today's promise:
God laid *your* sins on Christ.

# SEPTEMBER 20

Matthew 7:24–25, NASB:
"Therefore everyone who hears these words of Mine and acts on them, may be compared to a wise man who built his house on the rock. And the rain fell, and the floods came, and the winds blew and slammed against that house; and yet it did not fall, for it had been founded on the rock."

---

I was in Hurricane Ike, which hit Galveston, Texas, and came up to my aunt's house on the shore of Galveston Bay. My aunt, my mother, and I took refuge at a hotel at Hobby Airport. The winds came. The rains fell. And the waters surged. Unfortunately, my aunt's house was flooded. However, some houses on her street (which had been built on elevated foundations) withstood the storm. They were not flooded, because they had the right foundation.

Our Lord says that His Word is a strong foundation. Today's truth-promise says that we have a choice: build our lives on the solid foundation of God's Word or build our lives on anything else and not be able to withstand the storms of life

—JGH

Today's promise:
God Word is a *solid* foundation.

# SEPTEMBER 21

Deuteronomy 31:8, KJV:
"And the Lord, he it is that doth go before thee; he will be with thee, he will not fail thee, neither forsake thee: fear not, neither be dismayed."

---

As one who is sincere and generous with her gratitude and praise, I confess that sometimes it's nice to hear that in return. (I've never done the "love language" thing that some of my friends are talking about, but I think that's mine—if that even is one; if not, they should add it!)

However, gratitude and praise can't be mustered up. The spoken word has to be genuine to matter. And today, I received exactly that. But it wasn't in the form that you might think. It was in eight amazing words (found in today's promise verse) that reminded me that there is a *constant* in the midst of everything else that is changing: "He will not fail thee, neither forsake thee."

He made me. He knows me. He cares. He gets it. He's invested in me. He won't fail me. He won't abandon me. He loves me unconditionally. He's the constant in a life filled with contrasts and changes.

Herein is love.

—BLH

Today's promise:
God will *never* fail you—ever!

# SEPTEMBER 22

1 John 5:19–20, NASB:
"We know that we are of God, and that the whole world lies in the power of the evil one. And we know that the Son of God has come, and has given us understanding so that we may know Him who is true; and we are in Him who is true, in His Son Jesus Christ."

---

At one time, I was a flight instructor, teaching people how to fly. I would describe a maneuver and tell the student how to do it. But here was the problem: I would overload the student with details, creating complexity instead of simplicity. Those who could explain the instructions in a simple "1–2–3" step were great instructors, and I wished I could teach like they did.

First John is a letter to believers as little children. John therefore keeps his instructions very simple, basic, and clear. In today's truth-promise, John states that: "God the Son has come," and that He "is true."

Additionally, John tells us that we have clear instructions on how we can personally know God the Son—through the understanding God has given us.

—JGH

Today's promise:
You are in Christ, Who is *true*.

# SEPTEMBER 23

Isaiah 42:8, KJV:
"I am the Lord: that is my name: and my glory will I not give to another, neither my praise to graven images."

---

What's in a name? Mine is Joseph Gustave Henderson, Jr. Yes, I'm a "junior." I was named after my dad, who is now with the Lord. My dad was called, "Gus"; I am called, "Joe."

I have trouble with names; that is, I can't recall names. When I do, I often use the wrong name. Don't you admire people who can not only remember a name but also use it correctly? It is important to people that you call them by the right name.

Today's truth-promise states that God's name ("the Lord") is important to Him. He *is* the Lord. Along with His name, God says that His glory (His splendor) He will "not give to another." God further says that His praise is important, and He will not give it to anything or anyone else.

—JGH

Today's promise:
God *is* the *Lord*!

# SEPTEMBER 24

Matthew 19:26, ESV:
"But Jesus looked at them and said, 'With man this is impossible, but with God all things are possible.'"

---

Too often when I look at potential I use it as a way of envisioning how *my* plans would look if they were carried out.

This very thing seemed to play out in the early verses of John chapter five: a man had been ill for thirty-eight years, and as he lay by the healing pool of Bethesda, he saw the potential that its water held. In fact, he even tried to avail himself of it to fulfill his own plan for healing but could never make it into the water on his own.

Then Jesus came! When the man received the power of Christ's healing, he was not only healed of his illness, but great options were now before him. Because he had the power of Christ, the potential of his plans turned into actual possibilities!

—BLH

Today's promise:
With God, all things *are* possible!

# SEPTEMBER 25

Ephesians 2:4–5, NASB:
"But God, being rich in mercy, because of His great love with which He loved us, even when we were dead in our transgressions, made us alive together with Christ
(by grace you have been saved)."

---

This chapter starts with Paul reminding his readers that at one time they had been spiritually dead because of their sins. Then comes today's truth-promise verses, starting with two of my mom's favorite words in Scripture: *But God*.

Through an incomparable contrast to our sinful state, God, with His abundance of mercy and His unconditional, unfailing love, raised us out of our spiritually dead state, just as He had raised His Own Son from the dead!

Paul adds in that powerful but concise reminder at the end, just to keep our thoughts on how drastically different God's grace is when held up next to our sins.

Blessed contrast! Abundant mercy!

—BLH

Today's promise:
God saved you by His *grace!*

# SEPTEMBER 26

Romans 8:38–39, KJV:
"For I am persuaded, that neither death, nor life, nor angels,
nor principalities, nor powers, nor things present,
nor things to come, nor height, nor depth, nor any other creature,
shall be able to separate us from the love of God,
which is in Christ Jesus our Lord."

---

Paul declared to the Romans that nothing can separate us from God's love, which is in Christ. To be separated from God's love would mean that we would be completely isolated from it.

Paul's list here is long. You could add *anything* to it. However, *anything* you add would still be *nothing*. And the truth-promise in this verse would remain: that *nothing* can take us away from God and His love.

—JGH

Today's promise:
*Nothing* can separate you from God's love!

# SEPTEMBER 27

1 Thessalonians 2:13, NASB:
"For this reason we also constantly thank God that when you received the word of God which you heard from us, you accepted it not as the word of men, but for what it really is, the word of God, which also performs its work in you who believe."

---

My father, who was also my pastor, was particularly intense one day in his preaching. He was driving home a point and raised his voice a little, emphasizing God's anger over our sin and then closing with the hope of eternal life that Christ's death offers as the only payment for that sin.

A young boy was walking out of the church service with his mom and said to her, "Wow! God was really mad today, wasn't he?"

We have teased him about that question several times through the years, but today his question made me think of this verse, even though its point is reversed.

Paul states in today's truth-promise that he is grateful that the church in Thessalonica knew that it was not their words as mere men that they were preaching and teaching, but that it was indeed the Word of God. He knew that they had accepted it as such, because it was doing what God's Word was intended to do: performing "its work" in their lives.

—BLH

Today's promise:
God's Word *will* carry out its intended purpose in you.

# SEPTEMBER 28

Psalm 145:20, NKJV:
"The Lord preserves all who love him,
but all the wicked he will destroy."

---

If you were to open your kitchen cupboards, you would most likely find food labels with lists of preservatives that were placed there by the manufacturers to keep the food from going bad for as long as possible. In fact, we sometimes take fresh fruits and make them into "preserves" so that they will last longer and can be enjoyed throughout the year.

So let's use those simple illustrations to help us see the true scope of what God does when He preserves us, noting that He promises to destroy (cast out) the wicked who do *not* accept His offer of adoption into the family of God (through faith in Christ alone):

- ➢ God preserves us from evil by providing a "way of escape" when temptations come our way. (See 1 Corinthians 10:13.)

- ➢ God preserves us as believers. We will remain His children for all eternity!

—BLH

Today's promise:
God *will* preserve you as His child!

# SEPTEMBER 29

Psalm 44:4, NKJV:
"For they did not gain possession of the land by their own sword, nor did their own arm save them; but it was Your right hand, Your arm, and the light of Your countenance, Because You favored them."

---

I find it fascinating to watch the interviews with the players following a televised sporting event. It's especially fun to watch when previously unknown players who make great plays during the game are interviewed for the first time. The exuberance on their faces speaks volumes—and so do their words. Some are truly team players, giving credit to their teammates and coaches for the preparation and team effort that enabled them to make the now-famous play. Others, sadly, talk of their own greatness quite freely, as though the points that were scored by others were inconsequential to the outcome of the game.

In today's truth-promise, the psalmist acknowledges to the Lord that the children of Israel had no claim on their victories. It was through God alone and His favor on them that they had defeated their enemies. His right hand of power and "the light of [His] countenance" were responsible.

"But He gives more grace. Therefore He says, 'God resists the proud, but gives grace to the humble'" (James 4:6, NKJV).

—BLH

Today's promise:
*God* gives the victory!

# SEPTEMBER 30

Psalm 18:31–32, ESV:
"For who is God, but the Lord? And who is a rock, except our God?—the God who equipped me with strength
and made my way blameless."

---

In our marriage, we each know that we take second place in the other's life. And we don't have a problem with that, because it is our amazing God Who takes first place in each of our lives!

Today's truth-promise verses take it a step further. The psalmist skillfully reminds us that there is no one like our God! He is incomparable in His person, His character, and His love.

And in keeping with Who He is and with the generosity of His grace, He uses His power and the magnitude of *His* strength to empower *us*!

And this, indeed, is love.

—JGH

Today's promise:
God *will* equip you with strength!

# OCTOBER 1

Psalm 106:1, NKJV:
"Praise the Lord! Oh, give thanks to the Lord, for He is good!
For His mercy endures forever."

---

We admonish our children to say, "Thank you" when someone does something for them or gives them something: "What do you say?" is the question we routinely ask. We all know the answer: "Thank you."

The psalmist could be asking us the "thank-you" question with his clear command: "Oh, give thanks unto the Lord." But today's truth-promise gives us the *why*: because of His eternal goodness and His eternal mercy.

—JGH

Today's promise:
The Lord is *eternally* good and merciful!

# OCTOBER 2

Psalm 34:9, ESV:
"Oh, fear the Lord, you His saints!
There is no want to those who fear Him."

———

Sometimes my "wanter" needs repairs. I want this. I want that. I don't want this. I don't want that. Sometimes I just plain don't know *what* I want!

The psalmist comforts our confused minds by reminding us, via today's truth-promise, to stand in awe of our amazing God. When we keep our eyes fixed on Him (see Hebrews 12:2), our wants are more easily aligned with His desires for us, and our "wanters" begin to recognize that God makes sure that what we need is not lacking. (See Psalm 23:1.)

—BLH

Today's promise:
God *will* take care of all that you truly need.

# OCTOBER 3

Luke 11:13, NASB:
"If you then, being evil, know how to give good gifts to your children, how much more will your heavenly Father give the Holy Spirit to those who ask Him?

---

Today is my daughter's birthday. As Anna's father, I enjoy giving her good gifts. But I'm not perfect; I am a sinner saved by God's grace.

Today's truth-promise shows a tremendous comparison and contrast: God, our heavenly Father, being absolutely good, gives us the Holy Spirit to live within us. Along with *that* wonderful Gift, He gives us:

His Word,
His grace,
His comfort,
His peace,
His guidance,
His provision,
...and so much more!

Truly—so much more!

—JGH

Today's promise:
God gives *good gifts* to His children!

# OCTOBER 4

1 John 2:15–17, AMP:
"Do not love the world [of sin that opposes God and His precepts], nor the things that are in the world. If anyone loves the world, the love of the Father is not in him. For all that is in the world—the lust and sensual craving of the flesh and the lust and longing of the eyes and the boastful pride of life [pretentious confidence in one's resources or in the stability of earthly things]—these do not come from the Father, but are from the world. The world is passing away, and with it its lusts [the shameful pursuits and ungodly longings]; but the one who does the will of God and carries out His purposes lives forever."

---

We tend to live for things—stuff that we see. But the "stuff" that we have here on earth will pass away.

Of course, we are *in* the world, and we have to deal with temporal things. But we should remember to live with eternity in view, doing the will of God in our hearts.

—JGH

Today's promise:
God desires for you to live with *eternity* in view!

# OCTOBER 5

Isaiah 12:2, KJV:
"Behold, God is my salvation; I will trust, and not be afraid: for the Lord Jehovah is my strength and my song; he also is become my salvation."

---

On this day, my birthday, we will celebrate! Another important day is coming—the day when I, along with all others, will stand before God. On that day, I will recall Isaiah 12—the chapter in Scripture that I have chosen as my "life chapter." In particular, I believe that I will recall today's truth-promise (which I many years ago chose as my "life verse"), Isaiah 12:2.

God *is* my salvation. I *have* trusted Him. I *will not* be afraid. He *is*, therefore, "my strength and my song."

Now *that* will be a day to celebrate!

—JGH

Today's promise:
God *is* your salvation!

# OCTOBER 6

Psalm 27:14, KJV:
"Wait on the Lord: be of good courage, and he shall strengthen thine heart: wait, I say, on the Lord."

---

In the verse that precedes this one, the psalmist writes, "I had fainted, unless I had believed to see the goodness of the Lord in the land of the living" (Psalm 27:13, KJV). He's confessing to us that he had reached a point where, if he had not seen God's good hand at work, he would have given up.

Then he follows that up with a reminder—"Wait on the Lord"—and a promise: "He shall strengthen thine heart." It's interesting to me that he recognizes our penchant to worry, because at the end of the verse he reminds us: "Wait, I say, on the Lord."

As you wait, He will empower you. Even when you think your spirit might "faint" or give up, wait on God.

As you wait, He will keep His promise to strengthen your heart.

As you wait with expectant hope, look for the goodness of the Lord. It *will* be there!

—BLH

Today's promise:
God *will* strengthen your heart.

# OCTOBER 7

1 Chronicles 28:9, ESV:
"And you, Solomon my son, know the God of your father and serve him with a whole heart and with a willing mind, for the Lord searches all hearts and understands every plan and thought. If you seek him, he will be found by you, but if you forsake him, he will cast you off forever."

---

David's words to his son Solomon could be spoken today by any father, mother, teacher, or friend and still ring true.

With great wisdom, David didn't just give his son the command, "Know God." He explained the *why*.

Because the Lord knows the motives and the plans of our hearts, He is the One Who should be sought and Who should be called upon to lead us. When our trust is in Him, causing us to keep our eyes on Him, we will desire to serve Him "with a whole heart and a willing mind."

—BLH

Today's promise:
God *knows* your heart, your plans, and your thoughts.

# OCTOBER 8

Jeremiah 14:22, AMP:
"Are there any among the idols of the nations who can send rain?
Or can the heavens [of their own will] give showers?
Is it not You, O Lord our God? Therefore we will wait and hope
[confidently] in You, For You are the one who has made
all these things [the heavens and the rain]."

---

God allowed me to fly airplanes for nearly fifty years. In that time, I flew in my fair share of rain showers.

Today's truth-promise states that rain showers come from God. However, God also takes the time here to say that false gods do not have the power to give weather.

Therefore, in all situations of life—not just those related to weather—we should expectantly look to God. (See Psalm 62:5.)

—JGH

Today's promise:
God made *all* things.

# OCTOBER 9

Mark 10:26–27, NKJV:
"And they were greatly astonished,
saying among themselves, 'Who then can be saved?'
But Jesus looked at them and said, 'With men it is impossible,
but not with God; for with God all things are possible.'"

---

In Mark 10, the true story is recorded of Jesus telling His followers that wealth could not be used to buy someone's way into heaven. They were, apparently, surprised by this fact and looked at each other, asking, "Who then can be saved?"

Don't you love Jesus's answer here? He tells it like it is in a very simple way: "With men it is impossible, but not with God."

Salvation comes by grace alone, through faith alone in Christ alone. No money, no good works, no Christian legacy of faith can earn us the joys of heaven. In and of ourselves, it is impossible.

But…"with God all things are possible!"

"Not by works of righteousness which we have done, but according to His mercy He saved us, through the washing of regeneration and renewing of the Holy Spirit" (Titus 3:5, NKJV).

—BLH

Today's promise:
Your salvation is *only* possible through the gift of God!

# OCTOBER 10

Proverbs 3:13, 15–17, KJV:
"Happy is the man that findeth wisdom, and the man that getteth understanding. She is more precious than rubies: and all the things thou canst desire are not to be compared unto her.
Length of days is in her right hand;
and in her left hand riches and honour.
Her ways are ways of pleasantness, and all her paths are peace."

---

It's interesting—and eye-opening—to observe the various ways that people live. The person without godly wisdom seeks anything and everything to fulfill his or her desires apart from God. The result is futility, unhappiness, and a dissatisfaction that is unfulfilling.

The person who begins with godly wisdom is promised immeasurable, valuable benefits. In addition to tangible benefits, godly wisdom yields serenity and peace that those without godly wisdom cannot enjoy.

—JGH

Today's promise:
God *will* bless those who obtain godly wisdom!

# OCTOBER 11

Psalm 97:1, NKJV:
"The Lord reigns; let the earth rejoice;
let the multitude of isles be glad!"

---

As airline pilots, we were admonished to keep the passengers informed. (As my wife, Brenda, likes to say, "Informed people are happy people!") We were to give our public-address announcements in a calm and clear manner so that passengers would know that someone was in charge and skillfully managing the flight.

Today's truth-promise clearly states that a righteous God in heaven is reigning, ruling, and overruling!

Later in this chapter (see Psalm 97:7), the psalmist states that idols—or things that people place above God—don't hear, speak, or do anything, and they bring confusion, not confirmation.

We can rejoice in God's righteous reign. As a dear pastor friend often reminds me: "God may be silent, but he is never still!"

—JGH

Today's promise:
God *is* in control!

# OCTOBER 12

Psalm 84:12, NKJV:
"O Lord of hosts, blessed is the man who trusts in You!"

---

Last year I had an annoying, lengthy bout with the flu, followed by a true case of the common cold—and all the joys that these comparatively minor illnesses carried with them! Joe was a patient and attentive caregiver, and I could not have been more grateful for his care. I not only counted on him to bring me juice, soup, and more tissues, but I found additional comfort in the mere fact that I *knew* that he would be there—helping, caring, providing, loving.

The simplicity of today's truth-promise speaks volumes! Its wonder lies not just in the fact—which is incredible!—that we can trust God. But in order to trust God, we have to *know* that we can trust Him.

This knowledge of God comes from learning about Him through our Bible reading and in-depth study of His Word, through devotional books likes this one, through the teaching of a Bible-believing church, and through the example of other believers—among other things God uses to teach us. As we come to know Him more deeply and more intimately, we know that we can trust Him to do what He says He will do and to be Who He says He will be!

And in so doing, we are blessed.

—BLH

Today's promise:
God *will* bless you for trusting in Him!

# OCTOBER 13

Isaiah 64:4, NKJV:
"For since the beginning of the world men have not heard nor perceived by the ear, nor has the eye seen any God besides You, Who acts for the one who waits for Him."

---

Think about this: God, the holy, mighty, powerful, omniscient creator of the universe, acts on your behalf. What He does is not for personal gain, but His actions spring from His unconditional, unending, unmerited love for you!

In reality, it's impossible to fathom that, isn't it? In today's truth-promise, Isaiah agrees. He declares that there is *no one* like our God—there never *has been*...nor will there *ever* be!

To use the currently popular expression: Wow! Just...wow!

—BLH

Today's promise:
Your incomparable God *will* act on your behalf!

# OCTOBER 14

Lamentations 3:24, NKJV:
"'The Lord is my portion,' says my soul,
'Therefore I hope in Him!'"

---

Often when we think of the word *portion* it conjures up thoughts of a cafeteria tray with portions of food doled out within the various sections of the tray. Or we may think of doing this at the end of a meal: taking the total amount and dividing it into portions so that each person can pay his or her portion of the total bill.

In today's truth-promise, the writer uses the word *portion* similarly to that used in Luke 15:11–12, when the prodigal son requested his *portion* of his father's money. In his case, he wanted his inheritance (his portion) ahead of his father's death.

The fact that the Lord is our portion (our inheritance) is hope-inducing for the writer—and for us! What we will gain is the Lord. He is the One we are longing for, living for, hoping for!

—BLH

Today's promise:
The *Lord* is your portion!

# OCTOBER 15

Daniel 2:20–21, NKJV:
"Daniel answered and said: 'Blessed be the name of God
forever and ever, for wisdom and might are His.
And He changes the times and the seasons; He removes kings and
raises up kings; He gives wisdom to the wise
and knowledge to those who have understanding.'"

---

Daniel needed to know King Nebuchadnezzar's dream. No other person had been able to accomplish this. However, Daniel not only needed to know what the dream had been; he also needed to explain its meaning.

Today's truth-promise is Daniel's praise and testimony about the Source of his wisdom—God. God had the wisdom and knowledge that Daniel needed, and God gave it to him.

He can do the same for you!

—JGH

Today's promise:
Wisdom comes from *God*.

# OCTOBER 16

Matthew 5:7, KJV:
"Blessed are the merciful: for they shall obtain mercy."

---

I knew of a lady who lived many years caring for an abusive, alcoholic husband. Her family marveled at her kind and compassionate treatment of him. Her consistent kindness, gracious demeanor, and forgiving disposition became well-known and appreciated within her community.

Instead of fighting back, she was merciful. She overcame evil behavior with goodness and mercy.

Was it easy for her to do this? No. Was it the life she would have chosen? No. However, God gave her an inexplicable joy and bestowed mercy on her, just as she had shown mercy to the undeserving.

—JGH

Today's promise:
God *will* bestow mercy on the merciful.

# OCTOBER 17

Psalm 32:8, ESV:
"I will instruct you and teach you in the way you should go;
I will counsel you with my eye upon you."

---

Joe and I oversee the bookstore at our church. It is open only a few times each week (before and after services), and it is skillfully run by a staff of volunteers.

When I joined Joe in this endeavor last year, I realized that several of the volunteers were uncomfortable with the computerized inventory and cash-register system. This wasn't caused by an inability to learn but because, although they had received instruction on the new equipment, their training hadn't included hands-on experience while the instructor was present.

In our first training session together, I had one of the volunteers come to the cash register, and while she rang up the pretend sale, I watched carefully and guided her, with my words, to the next step. She did it on her own, but I was there, watching and helping.

As the volunteers gain firsthand experience, their confidence grows by knowing that I'm nearby, ready to counsel them on how to accomplish the steps of the sales process. I don't do it *for* them; I teach *them* how to do it!

God wants us to be successful. That's why, with His eye upon us, He instructs us, teaches us, and counsels us to and through the next best step.

—BLH

Today's promise:
He *will* instruct you, teach you, counsel you.

# OCTOBER 18

John 17:17, AMP:
"Sanctify them in the truth [set them apart for Your purposes, make them holy]; Your word is truth."

---

Today's truth-promise gives both a promise and a process that are accomplished by God's Word.

Scripture is absolute truth because it comes to us from God, Who *is* truth. What God wants for us is change. This change is for us to become purified, set apart, and holy for His purposes and use. He will do this through His Word, which we can read, receive, and apply to our lives.

—JGH

Today's promise:
God's Word is *truth*.

# OCTOBER 19

Galatians 3:13, AMP:
"Christ purchased our freedom and redeemed us
from the curse of the Law and its condemnation by becoming a
curse for us—for it is written,
'Cursed is everyone who hangs [crucified] on a tree (cross).'"

---

This glorious truth-promise should restore to all believers the joy of their salvation! (See Psalm 51:12.) Take a moment today to ponder the curse of death that Christ willingly suffered so that you could be delivered from sin's curse.

He purchased your eternal freedom! He redeemed you from the curse of the Law—and its condemnation!

Glorious truth.

Glorious promise!

—BLH

Today's promise:
Christ's death *released* you from the curse of sin!

# OCTOBER 20

Ephesians 1:7–8, NASB:
"In Him we have redemption through His blood,
the forgiveness of our trespasses, according to the riches of His grace which He lavished on us...."

---

As if the thought that we have redemption through His blood isn't enough to just plain knock our socks off, that expression, "which He lavished on us," is probably one of the best descriptions in all of word-dom!

Doesn't that just conjure up the mental picture of grace upon grace upon grace upon...! We don't earn it. It's just this unfounded, incomparable, beyond-generous grace that He *lavishes* on us!

Best word ever!

Carry that thought today: you are, at every moment, being "bestowed profusely" (*Merriam-Webster Dictionary*) with His grace!

What possible sin can that grace not redeem?

What possible sincere need can that grace not supply?

What possible problem can that grace not handle?

—BLH

Today's promise:
He *will* lavish His grace on you!

# OCTOBER 21

Psalm 29:11, AMP:
"The Lord will give [unyielding and impenetrable] strength to His people; the Lord will bless His people with peace."

---

Don't you love those words: *unyielding and impenetrable*? My strength fails so easily. It dims, and my spirit grows weak. That is when the fears, worries, what-ifs, and anxiousness rise to the top of my emotional responses.

But the strength that God gives carries with it a staying power that results in a peace-filled, calm heart that rests—because it trusts.

—BLH

Today's promise:
God *will* give you "unyielding and impenetrable" strength!

# OCTOBER 22

Psalm 31:22, AMP:
"As for me, I said in my alarm, 'I am cut off from Your eyes.' Nevertheless You heard the voice of my supplications (specific requests) when I cried to You [for help]."

---

The psalmist had some pretty hateful enemies. They literally sought to destroy—and even *end*—his life. So it is more than understandable that he had moments of alarm! We all would! But in his alarm, He had questioned the presence of God, and that is what he is confessing here.

Then he added that beautiful word: *Nevertheless*. He was smitten with wonder at the fact that in spite of his lapse in trust, God had heard his voice and had answered his "specific requests."

Mercy upon mercy. Eternal, unchanging mercy, still available and freely given to us today!

—JGH

Today's promise:
God *will* hear your specific requests!

# OCTOBER 23

1 John 2:1–2, AMP:
"My little children (believers, dear ones), I am writing you these things so that you will not sin and violate God's law. And if anyone sins, we have an Advocate [who will intercede for us] with the Father: Jesus Christ the righteous [the upright, the just One, who conforms to the Father's will in every way—purpose, thought, and action]. And He [that same Jesus] is the propitiation for our sins [the atoning sacrifice that holds back the wrath of God that would otherwise be directed at us because of our sinful nature—our worldliness, our lifestyle]; and not for ours alone, but also for [the sins of all believers throughout] the whole world."

---

An advocate is a person who pleads on behalf of or supports another's cause, often via the role of a lawyer in a court of law. These verses tell us that Christ is our Advocate!

Following our salvation, when we sin, God (as our Father) disciplines us as His children, not as condemned sinners. Not only do we have the blessing of His forgiveness when we confess our sins (see 1 John 1:9), but Christ, our Advocate, intercedes on our behalf to the Father!

—JGH

Today's promise:
Christ *will* be your Advocate with the Father!

# OCTOBER 24

Psalm 73:24, NKJV:
"You will guide me with Your counsel,
And afterward receive me to glory."

---

We often speak of God's omnipresence and find comfort in knowing that God is "all present." But do we truly get what that means? I think this verse sums it up beautifully.

When we go to a museum, our guide walks with us through the exhibits, carefully explaining each one and helping us understand the things that are not familiar to us.

When we go whitewater rafting, our guide is in the raft with us, teaching us how to navigate the uncertain waters that we are traveling.

In life, our Guide is there—ever present, ever with us. He counsels us, knowing that the path we are walking is unfamiliar and uncertain.

But God's omnipresence as our Guide doesn't end with our journey on this earth. He also will be present with us when we leave this world and enter heaven's splendor. In fact, He will be there to receive us into glory.

Wherever we are today, whatever unfamiliar and uncertain path we may be walking, He is there.

—BLH

Today's promise:
He *will* guide you, because He is there!

# OCTOBER 25

John 4:14, KJV:
"But whoever drinks of the water that I shall give him will never thirst. But the water that I shall give him will become in him a fountain of water springing up into everlasting life."

---

On the farm in Arkansas where my dad grew up, there are many rice fields. These fields need large amounts of water and are filled by artesian wells. These wells powerfully and continuously pump water into the fields. The water is clear, fresh, and gushing freely.

God's salvation in Christ has been described as a well of water (Isaiah 12:3). Just as in an artesian well, God's well of salvation powerfully saves, sustains, refreshes, cleanses—and never runs dry.

—JGH

Today's promise:
His water of salvation *will* quench your spiritual thirst.

# OCTOBER 26

Acts 17:24–25, ESV:
"The God who made the world and everything in it, being Lord of heaven and earth, does not live in temples made by man, nor is he served by human hands, as though he needed anything, since he himself gives to all mankind life and breath and everything."

———

The apostle Paul was confronting "religious" men regarding the idols they were worshipping. He chose one of the best possible methods to do that: he contrasted their gods with the one true God.

In the verses from which we glean today's truth-promise, Paul started by making the very clear point that God "made the world and everything in it." This included the materials from which the idols had been carved or created!

Next, Paul pointed out that God didn't live in an earthly temple, crafted by humans.

He concluded by opening their eyes to the fact that even though their idols had to be fed or bribed (or other actions from humans to the gods), the living God didn't need anything from humans, because, after all, He had created them!

—BLH

Today's promise:
God made the world and *everything* in it!

# OCTOBER 27

1 Timothy 2:5–6, NASB:
"For there is one God, and one mediator also between God and men, the man Christ Jesus, who gave Himself as a ransom for all, the testimony given at the proper time."

---

When two or more people, groups, or organizations are at odds with one another, a mediator is called to step in and is there to bring the two parties together. Today's truth-promise sets forth the role of Jesus Christ as the mediator between God and humankind.

Christ mediates in order to bring sinners together with a holy God. He does so, as only Christ could, by paying the ransom that a righteous and holy God requires.

—JGH

Today's promise:
Christ *is* your mediator!

# OCTOBER 28

Jeremiah 9:23–24, NKJV:
"Thus says the Lord: 'Let not the wise man glory in his wisdom, let not the mighty man glory in his might, nor let the rich man glory in his riches; but let him who glories glory in this, that he understands and knows Me, that I am the Lord, exercising lovingkindness, judgment, and righteousness in the earth. For in these I delight,' says the Lord."

---

The Lord used the prophet Jeremiah to teach His people some very important lessons. The truth-promise Jeremiah shared in today's verses is one that we can benefit from as well.

God says:

Are you boasting about your wisdom? Don't. You got it from Me.
Are you boasting about your power? Don't. You got it from Me.
Are you boasting about your wealth? Don't. You got it from Me.

Do you need something to glory in? Glory in the fact that you know Me, and that you know that I am the merciful, righteous Judge of the earth.

—BLH

Today's promise:
God *is* the Lord of the earth!

# OCTOBER 29

Revelation 21:4, KJV:
"And God shall wipe away all tears from their eyes; and there shall be no more death, neither sorrow, nor crying, neither shall there be any more pain: for the former things are passed away."

---

God, in His love for John the apostle and for us, gave the book of Revelation to tell us things that were, that are, and that will be (see Revelation 1:19).

In the New Jerusalem that John saw coming down from heaven, there were a number of things that John said will not be there: there will be no more tears, death, sorrow, crying, or pain.

However, God *will* be there! And He will wipe away all tears!

Do you remember when your parents would wipe away your tears? It made everything better. In that wonderful day, your heavenly Father will wipe your tears away, and all will be well.

—JGH

Today's promise:
God *will* wipe your tears away!

# OCTOBER 30

Psalm 145:8, KJV:
"The Lord is gracious, and full of compassion;
slow to anger, and of great mercy."

---

When you read a truth-promise like today's verse, it's easy to focus on the four descriptions of God: gracious, full of compassion, slow to anger, of great mercy. All of them are wonderful!

Today however, I'd like you to "major on the minors." In other words, think about a word that, at first glance, doesn't seem to be all that significant: *full*.

Our Lord is *full* of compassion. *Full*! I don't even need to check an official dictionary to understand that one! *Full*—as in not room for any more! And our amazing God is full of compassion! That's as compassionate as it gets!

And when I think of that, I'm *filled* with gratitude!

—BLH

Today's promise:
The Lord is *full* of compassion!

# OCTOBER 31

Psalm 92:5, AMP:
"How great are Your works, O Lord!
Your thoughts are very deep [beyond man's understanding]."

---

A friend was trying to explain a rather complicated concept to me, and I was certain that the blank stare on my face would betray my total lack of understanding. Seriously, she could have been speaking in Swahili for all I knew—or didn't know!

I finally held up my hand in a request for her to pause and said, "I'm smart; I'm just not very deep. Would you please explain this again with that in mind?"

We both got a good chuckle out it, and I even ended up with at least a *slight* understanding of our conversation!

But oh, my friend, how truly deep God's thoughts are. They are, as our truth-promise states, "beyond [our] understanding." What He knows is infinite in its breadth, height, and depth.

Yet so often we try to figure out the *whys* that only God knows. Instead, perhaps we should say, "I don't understand, but You do. And since You know all things, I will trust Your plan."

—BLH

Today's promise:
God's thoughts are *beyond* your understanding.

# NOVEMBER 1

Jeremiah 32:27, NKJV:
"Behold, I am the Lord, the God of all flesh.
Is there anything too hard for Me?"

---

*Wikipedia* defines a rhetorical question as: "a figure of speech in the form of a question that is asked to make a point rather than to elicit an answer."

Previously in this chapter from Jeremiah, he had stated (in Jeremiah 32:17, KJV): "there is nothing too hard for Thee." Jeremiah knew that God was the creator God, and His very act of creation had proven that He could do anything.

In today's truth-promise, God is asking a rhetorical question, driving home the point that no, there is nothing that is too hard for Him. God simply added that He is the God Who created all beings—in addition to the heavens and the earth that Jeremiah had mentioned in verse 17.

Try to wrap your mind around that if you can—He stated it twice in one chapter to help you do that: Nothing...not one thing...is too hard for God!

—BLH

Today's promise:
*Nothing* is too hard for God!

# NOVEMBER 2

James 4:7, KJV:
"Submit yourselves therefore to God. Resist the devil, and he will flee from you."

---

On January 1, we laid the foundation for all of the promises that would follow: "God *cannot* lie!" It has been true. It is true. And it will continue to be true, long after you finish reading this year-long devotional book. As we look together at today's promise, I think that it's important for us to remember that fact.

When I read James 4:7, I was trying to find more "steps" for us to take in order to get the evil ick to leave us alone. Surely His promise couldn't be that simple on this end.

But God, Who cannot lie, said that what we need to do to get the devil to run from us is to resist him. And then, our powerful, omniscient God promises us that Satan will flee!

So if I'm having a sin issue rear its ugly head over and over again, the problem isn't that God can't handle it; it's that I'm not resisting. Oh, I may think that I am, but if I were truly resisting the onslaughts of the evil ick, he would be headed off to pester someone else.

No more, Mr. Satan. I'm in "resistance mode!"

—BLH

Today's promise:
If you resist the devil, he *will* flee from you!

# NOVEMBER 3

Psalm 102:27, NKJV:
"But You are the same, and Your years will have no end."

———

How do you comprehend eternity? How do you understand God, Who lives in eternity? (See Isaiah 57:17.) How do you grasp the thought that Someone does not change for eternity?

The answer to each of these questions is the same: You don't, and you can't.

But you *can* believe in an eternal God—and believe that He is an eternal God Who does not change. You *can* believe that this eternal and unchanging God loves *you*.

—JGH

Today's promise:
God *is eternal*!

# NOVEMBER 4

Colossians 3:1, AMP:
"Therefore if you have been raised with Christ
[to a new life, sharing in His resurrection from the dead],
keep seeking the things that are above, where Christ is,
seated at the right hand of God."

---

As we were studying the various promises and truth-promises for this book, we kept coming across references to God's right hand. After some additional research and study, we were able to learn that the mention of God's right hand implies two things: His power and His giving honor to the recipient of that specific action (seating Someone at His right hand; extending His right hand).

Christ, His precious Son, after He was raised from His death here on earth, ascended into heaven to be with the Father. The truth-promise that Jesus is now seated at God's right hand tells us that God honored Him and considered Christ His equal.

What a wonderful comfort it is to know today that our Advocate is seated right next to—and honored by—the Judge!

—BLH

Today's promise:
Christ *is* in heaven, at God's right hand.

# NOVEMBER 5

Psalm 81:10, NKJV:
"I am the Lord your God, Who brought you out of the land of Egypt; open your mouth wide, and I will fill it."

---

Though this was a promise to the children of Israel, it is very much a truth-promise for us today. Our unchanging God has not changed even one little bit since He first uttered these words, and He still longs to give good things to His children (see Matthew 7:11).

Just as He promised in this verse to fill their wide-open mouths (implying that He would provide more than enough), He has promised us this wonderful gift as well. In fact, He told us in Ephesians 3:20 (AMP) that He would do "superabundantly more than all that we dare ask or think [infinitely beyond our greatest prayers, hopes, or dreams]."

Now that's what I call more than enough!

—BLH

Today's promise:
God's provision is *more* than enough!

# NOVEMBER 6

Hebrews 4:16, AMP:
"Therefore let us [with privilege] approach the throne of grace [that is, the throne of God's gracious favor] with confidence and without fear, so that we may receive mercy [for our failures] and find [His amazing] grace to help in time of need [an appropriate blessing, coming just at the right moment]."

---

Today's truth-promise is a wonderful and powerful appeal for us to pray to God our Father. God is a gracious and merciful God; therefore, His seat of rule is a throne of mercy and grace.

We need God's mercy through the forgiveness of our sins and through His pity and kindness. We also need His grace. God's grace can be seen in His promise of sufficient help.

Whatever our need—physical, emotional, or spiritual—there is a Person (our gracious, merciful God), and there is a place where we can confidently go in prayer for our needs.

—JGH

Today's promise:
You *will* receive mercy and grace at God's throne.

# NOVEMBER 7

Proverbs 14:26, KJV:
"In the fear of the Lord is strong confidence:
and his children shall have a place of refuge."

---

As you stand in awe of God today (by soaking in the truths of His Word and meditating on Who He is), you will have confidence—no, *strong* confidence—in His ability to keep His promises.

I encourage you to take a few extra moments today to look back through some of your favorite promises from previous months and review in your mind (or share with a friend) how God has kept His Word.

Therein is a place of refuge.

—BLH

Today's promise:
God provides a *refuge* for you when you stand in awe of Him!

# NOVEMBER 8

Psalm 86:7, KJV:
"In the day of my trouble I will call upon thee:
for thou wilt answer me."

———

Perhaps the fact that I've been guilty of it myself (though I really try *not* to do it) makes me more frustrated with others who do the same thing: not sending a reply to an invitation or an e-mail. That frustration level increases for all of us when we're seeking help, assistance, or an answer to a pressing need—and the answer never arrives.

But the psalmist has a calm assurance that when trouble comes, he can call on the Lord. He knows that the Lord will answer Him. When you know beyond a doubt that the recipient of your request will answer, you don't mind waiting. In fact, you trust that the listener's delays are there because he or she is waiting in order to be able to provide you with the best possible answer.

We serve the God of the psalmist. God cares about our troubles. He listens when we cry out for His help and comfort. He will answer!

—BLH

Today's promise:
God *will* answer!

# NOVEMBER 9

Luke 11:28, NASB:
"But He said, 'On the contrary, blessed are those who hear the word of God and observe it.'"

---

Don't you just find it amazing that God not only gave His Word, the Bible, to provide everything you need for life and godliness (see 2 Peter 1:3), but that He also *blesses* you for acting on its commands and applying its truths?

—BLH

Today's promise:
God *will* bless you for hearing and applying His Word!

# NOVEMBER 10

Matthew 5:6, AMP:
"Blessed [joyful, nourished by God's goodness] are those who hunger and thirst for righteousness [those who actively seek right standing with God], for they will be [completely] satisfied."

---

I know of runners who painstakingly train for marathons or races. I also know of athletes who eat special diets to build muscles and to increase their endurance levels for competition. This training often includes denying the athlete of certain foods and liquids. All of this effort is put forth in order to reach a goal and involves intense hunger and thirst.

God speaks in His Word of His ability to quench our spiritual thirst:

> "Therefore with joy shall ye draw water out of the wells of salvation" (Isaiah 12:3, KJV).

> "They drink their fill of the abundance of Your house;
> And You allow them to drink from the river of Your delights" (Psalm 36:8, AMP).

In today's verse, God declares that if we "actively seek" a right standing with Him, we will be "completely satisfied."

—JGH

Today's promise:
God *will* satisfy those who hunger and thirst for righteousness!

# NOVEMBER 11

Psalm 121:5, NKJV:
"The Lord is your keeper;
The Lord is your shade at your right hand."

---

Whenever God's names or attributes are mentioned in Scripture, they can also be seen as His promises. Because He is true to His name, He is true to the meanings of those names, thereby true to the promises that those names represent.

The fact that God is your keeper is pretty basic in its meaning. He keeps you, preserves you as His own, and surrounds you with the care that will protect you.

As one who has the Lord as your shade, you are again protected from harm, as this description would indicate. If He is close enough to shade you (or even to be your shadow, as some commentators believe this word to mean) then He is very, very close.

Oh, what precious promises are yours through His protection and His proximity!

—BLH

Today's promise:
The Lord *is* your keeper!

# NOVEMBER 12

1 John 4:18–19, NKJV:
"There is no fear in love; but perfect love casts out fear, because fear involves torment. But he who fears has not been made perfect in love. We love Him because He first loved us."

---

In the Garden of Eden, after Adam and Eve sinned, they were afraid of God. Their fear brought torment, and they hid from God. Sin separated them from their fellowship with God, and it does the same to us.

But God, Who is perfect love, sent the Lord Jesus Christ, His only Son, to die on the cross for our sins. Since we have trusted Christ and are reconciled to God, we should not be afraid of Him. We should instead love Him, Who first loved us.

—JGH

Today's promise:
God's *perfect love* casts out fear!

# NOVEMBER 13

2 Chronicles 20:6, ESV:
"And said, "O Lord, God of our fathers, are you not God in heaven? You rule over all the kingdoms of the nations. In your hand are power and might, so that none is able to withstand you."

---

King Jehoshaphat's enemies were on their way, intent to destroy him. Though he was indeed humanly fearful, he sought the Lord in prayer, and today's truth-promise is found in that prayer.

Actually, we need to follow Jehoshaphat's example of going to the Lord and acknowledging that He is the One Whose power and might we need fighting for us when trials come.

Don't think that because you aren't fighting a literal army your problems don't matter to God. Yes, He rules over "all the kingdoms of the nations," but within those kingdoms and nations are people—people just like you, confronted with everyday problems—who are to seek His guidance and strength.

—BLH

Today's promise:
In God's hand are *power* and *strength*!

# NOVEMBER 14

Matthew 10:29–31, NASB:
"Are not two sparrows sold for a cent? And yet
not one of them will fall to the ground apart from your Father.
But the very hairs of your head are all numbered.
So do not fear; you are more valuable than many sparrows."

---

I could write pages and pages about these three little verses, but no matter how hard I tried, I wouldn't be able to summarize the truth-promise in these verses any better than this:

You matter to God!

—BLH

Today's promise:
You *are* valuable to God!

# NOVEMBER 15

Psalm 62:8, KJV:
"Trust in him at all times; ye people, pour out your heart before him: God is a refuge for us."

---

I'm not a good listener. Too often, I'm not focused on the person talking to me. Too often, I'm thinking ahead of the person talking and frequently interjecting my thoughts into the unfinished conversation.

Today's truth-promise wonderfully declares that God is a good listener. He is able to listen to us all the time. He is able to hear our innermost thoughts and feelings—again, all the time.

Because He is a good listener, He is a help and shelter for us at all times!

—JGH

Today's promise:
God *is* a good listener!

# NOVEMBER 16

Isaiah 55:9, KJV:
"For as the heavens are higher than the earth, so are my ways higher than your ways, and my thoughts than your thoughts."

---

Aren't you glad that you and God don't think alike? Aren't you glad that His ways are not your ways?

Those may sound like strange questions, but I hope that your answer is *yes* to both of those. I realize that we are to have the mind of Christ (see Philippians 2:5), but according to today's truth-promise, we also can never fully know His thoughts or His ways. He sees the entire big picture and knows the who, the what, the where, the when, and the why of everything that has happened, is happening, or will happen.

After all, He is God.

—BLH

Today's promise:
God *is* omniscient (all-knowing)!

# NOVEMBER 17

Isaiah 30:15, NKJV:
"For thus says the Lord God, the Holy One of Israel:
'In returning and rest you shall be saved; in quietness and confidence shall be your strength.' But you would not."

———

In today's truth-promise, God was speaking through the prophet Isaiah to reach the "rebellious children." (See Isaiah 30:1.) The promise in this verse is amazing: they could return to Him and find rest, quietness of spirit, and strength-giving confidence. That's quite a promise—particularly to people who were rebelling against His ways.

The choice they made was made clear in the last four words—those sad four words—of this verse: "But you would not."

Don't miss out on the promises of God by choosing things or people that will distract you from keeping your focus on Him.

—BLH

Today's promise:
God *wants* you to choose to accept His blessings!

# NOVEMBER 18

Proverbs 19:21, ESV:
"Many are the plans in the mind of a man,
but it is the purpose of the Lord that will stand."

———

I have a calendar that includes a daily schedule, a weekly schedule, and a monthly schedule. It's color-coded and looks quite impressive, if I do say so myself. However, much to my chagrin, there are very, very few weeks and even days that truly follow that very ideal schedule. Why? Life happens.

On a much larger scale, today's truth-promise tells us not to be surprised by changes to our schedules, goals, and plans. God has a plan for each of us, and His plans have a purpose far greater than even our highest dreams and loftiest goals.

God's plans are best. His way is perfect.

—BLH

Today's promise:
God's plans and purposes *will not* fail!

# NOVEMBER 19

Jeremiah 10:10, AMP:
"But the Lord is the true God and the God who is Truth;
He is the living God and the everlasting King.
The earth quakes and shudders at His wrath,
and the nations are not able to endure His indignation."

---

Don't you love how the Amplified Bible starts today's truth-promise? "But the Lord is the true God and the God who is Truth."

He is not only the true (real) God—as opposed to the false idols and graven images that the people of Jeremiah's day were all too familiar with. He is also the God Who is Himself absolute truth! As we saw in January 1's promise: God *cannot* lie.

As if that weren't enough, Jeremiah blesses us with additional truth-promise descriptions about the God of truth:

- He is the living God.
- He is the everlasting King.
- The earth quakes at His wrath.
- The nations cannot endure His indignation.

Gratitude is not enough. This great God also deserves our worship, adoration, and devotion!

—BLH

Today's promise:
God *is* the God of truth!

# NOVEMBER 20

Jeremiah 17:7–8, ESV:
"Blessed is the man who trusts in the Lord, whose trust is
the Lord. He is like a tree planted by water,
that sends out its roots by the stream, and does not fear when heat
comes, for its leaves remain green, and is not anxious in the year
of drought, for it does not cease to bear fruit."

---

When the income decreases—or ceases;
when the second opinion is the same as the first;
when dreams are crushed;
when hope grows dim...

...trust in God.

Trust in God (true, deep-rooted, unshakable trust) doesn't fear when the unexpected happens.

That's why the writer said it twice—to reiterate the fact that our trust is not to be in people, things, or circumstances. Trust that is placed in the Lord is the trust that will be blessed.

—BLH

Today's promise:
God *will* bless you when you trust in Him!

# NOVEMBER 21

Romans 6:14, AMP:
"For sin will no longer be a master over you, since you are not under Law [as slaves], but under [unmerited] grace [as recipients of God's favor and mercy]."

---

Many things occur in us and for us when we trust Christ as our personal Savior. We are born again into a family—God's family. We are placed into Christ as members of His body, receiving eternal life and a home in heaven. We are placed in a new dominion—God's kingdom of light—and no longer dwell in the devil's kingdom of darkness.

Today's verse tells us that those who are in Christ are no longer slaves to sin but subjects under (and in the service of) God. Therefore, believers are not to obey sin but are to obey God, because sin no longer has control over them.

A family friend, Ken Collier, often says, "Just two choices on the shelf: pleasing God or pleasing self."

Who will you choose to follow today?

—JGH

Today's promise:
As God's child, you *no longer* have to yield to sin!

# NOVEMBER 22

Jeremiah 10:6, ESV:
"There is none like you, O Lord;
you are great, and your name is great in might."

---

In the opening verses of this chapter, Jeremiah shared God's words with the people, warning them against the futility of worshipping pagan idols. He didn't mince words:

> For the customs of the peoples are vanity. A tree from the forest is cut down and worked with an axe by the hands of a craftsman. They decorate it with silver and gold; they fasten it with hammer and nails so that it cannot move. Their idols are like scarecrows in a cucumber field, and they cannot speak; they have to be carried, for they cannot walk. Do not be afraid of them, for they cannot do evil, neither is it in them to do good.
> —Jeremiah 10:2–5, ESV

Jeremiah's immediate reaction to this description of their "handmade gods" was the prayer that is recorded for us in verse 6, which is today's truth-promise: "There is none like you, O Lord." Jeremiah not only knew that God was great, but that there was great might in His very name.

Today, thousands of years after the days of Jeremiah, there is still no one like our God. No one!

—BLH

Today's promise:
There is *no one* like our God!

# NOVEMBER 23

Psalm 92:12–15, AMP:
"The righteous will flourish like the date palm [long-lived, upright and useful]; they will grow like a cedar in Lebanon [majestic and stable]. Planted in the house of the Lord, they will flourish in the courts of our God. [Growing in grace] they will still thrive and bear fruit and prosper in old age; they will flourish and be vital and fresh [rich in trust and love and contentment];
[They are living memorials] to declare that the Lord is upright and faithful [to His promises]; He is my rock, and there is no unrighteousness in Him."

---

The word pictures the psalmist uses here are beautiful. These thriving trees represent the people who are known by the writer as being righteous individuals. Their characteristics are so skillfully mirrored by their plant-life counterparts:

- Long-lived
- Upright
- Useful
- Majestic
- Flourishing
- Growing (in grace)
- Thriving
- Bearing fruit
- Prospering (even in old age)
- Vital
- Rich (in trust and contentment)

Their purpose? To serve as "living memorials" to the fact that our sinless Rock is faithful to His promises.

—BLH

Today's promise:
God *is* faithful to His promises!

# NOVEMBER 24

John 15:15, NKJV:
"No longer do I call you servants, for a servant does not know what his master is doing; but I have called you friends, for all things that I heard from My Father I have made known to you."

---

Friendship is a deeper relationship than, say, the employer–employee relationship. Friends know each other well.

Friends share with each other. In today's truth-promise, our Lord says that everything He has heard from His Father, He has shared with us, His friends.

Friends help each other and bear each other's burdens.

Friends enjoy each other.

Friends love each other.

The hymnwriter got it right: "What a Friend We Have in Jesus!"

—JGH

Today's promise:
Jesus calls *you* His friend.

# NOVEMBER 25

Jeremiah 27:5, NKJV:
"I have made the earth, the man and the beast that are on the ground, by My great power and by My outstretched arm, and have given it to whom it seemed proper to Me."

---

Dr. John Whitcomb, well-known creationist, prolific author, and our family friend, will often come up to me and ask, "Brenda, how long did it take God to create the stars?"

I've learned by this time to join him in his speedy reply. So simultaneously we will click our tongue against the roof of our mouth and immediately say together, "Even that was too long!"

Think about that. God merely spoke, and there they were!

In today's truth-promise, God Himself reminds us that it was by His "great power and…outstretched arm" that He made "the earth, the man and the beast."

Surely He can take care of you!

—BLH

Today's promise:
Your powerful creator God *can* take care of you!

# NOVEMBER 26

Romans 2:11, AMP:
"For God shows no partiality [no arbitrary favoritism; with Him one person is not more important than another].

---

We live in a world of inequality. People often treat others unfairly, unequally, and unjustly. Some people receive extra privilege, position, and pay; others are hindered from advancement and equal pay.

However, today's truth-promise tells us that God is absolutely fair in His justice! He will always do right—not only in His justice but also in His blessings.

We may not understand or comprehend His ways, but we can trust Him to show no partiality! (See also Deuteronomy 32:4.) Thankfully, His blessings are not only abundant, but they are graciously given to all!

—JGH

Today's promise:
God is *impartial*!

# NOVEMBER 27

John 10:10, NASB:
"The thief comes only to steal and kill and destroy;
I came that they may have life, and have it abundantly."

---

Jesus is teaching the Parable of the Good Shepherd in this chapter. He paints various scenarios to teach scriptural truths so that His listeners can easily understand the lessons.

In today's truth-promise, Jesus reminded His listeners (including us) that His purpose in being on earth was only for their good. He desired for them to have a blessed life—and to have those blessings in abundance.

In this month when we typically set aside time to express our gratitude and count our blessings, I encourage you to take time today to thank God for your abundant blessings (even if they don't feel very abundant at times)!

—BLH

Today's promise:
God desires for you to have an *abundant* life!

# NOVEMBER 28

Lamentations 3:25, NKJV:
"The Lord is good to those who wait for Him,
to the soul who seeks Him."

---

Two activities are mentioned in today's truth-promise: waiting and seeking. Sometimes we wait in place. Perhaps we are waiting for direction or for answers to specific prayers. Perhaps we are being alert for His coming. At other times, we may be actively seeking or looking for the Lord.

For those who wait, God will strengthen them. (See Psalm 27:14.) For those who seek Him, He will be found. (See Jeremiah 10:13.) And to those who are waiting and seeking, God is good.

—JGH

Today's promise:
God *is* good.

# NOVEMBER 29

Psalm 51:6, AMP:
"Behold, You desire truth in the innermost being,
And in the hidden part [of my heart]
You will make me know wisdom."

———

They're called "spoiler alerts." It's when, let's say, you're attending a birthday party for your grandma, so you miss your favorite Olympic event but set your TV to record the competition so that you can watch it later. You return home just in time for the evening news, and they announce, "Spoiler alert! If you don't want to know the results of today's Olympic events, put your TV on mute in three seconds. Three…two…." And you mute your TV or put your fingers in your ears, while loudly and melodically saying, "Lalalalala—I can't heeeear you" in order not to hear what you really want to know.

I was recently supposed to read Psalm 51 as part of my daily Bible reading. However, I did not want to have those words prick my needy heart, so I closed my spiritual ears and nonverbally demonstrated a spirit of "Lalalalala—I can't heeeear you." I became obsessed with color coding the chapter, looking for "key words," and methodically performing my otherwise well-motivated Bible study habits in order to drown out the words I needed to "hear."

Yet, in His mercy, the Lord patiently spoke. And as His words began to reach their target audience—the depths of my heart—I clasped my hands together in a prayer of repentance for my unwillingness to listen to the spiritual wisdom my Lord wanted me to hear.

—BLH

Today's promise:
The Lord *will* give you spiritual wisdom!

# NOVEMBER 30

Revelation 1:3, KJV:
"Blessed is he that readeth, and they that hear the words of this prophecy, and keep those things which are written therein: for the time is at hand."

---

The Word of God is a letter from God to us. It is living, illuminating, powerful, and penetrating. (See Hebrews 4:12.) Today's truth-promise tells us of a certain and special happiness that will come from reading, hearing, and heeding the book of Revelation (the last book in the Bible).

While we do not fully understand all of Revelation, when we give attention to it, God will help our understanding and will bless us with its truths.

—JGH

Today's promise:
God *will* bless the reading of His Word!

# DECEMBER 1

Hebrews 13:20–21, NASB:
"Now the God of peace, who brought up from the dead the great Shepherd of the sheep through the blood of the eternal covenant, even Jesus our Lord, equip you in every good thing to do His will, working in us that which is pleasing in His sight, through Jesus Christ, to whom be the glory forever and ever. Amen."

---

God was able to raise His Son, Jesus, from the dead. Think about the wonder embodied in that fact for a moment.

The same God Who did that can certainly equip you to accomplish His will. There is no problem that He cannot solve, no need He cannot supply, no heart's cry that He cannot hear.

—BLH

Today's promise:
God *will* equip you to do His will!

# DECEMBER 2

Psalm 51:7, KJV:
"Purge me with hyssop, and I shall be clean:
wash me, and I shall be whiter than snow."

---

A former neighbor would often tease me about shoveling after only three inches of snow had fallen. "Hey, Brenda—you know we're still gonna get five more inches, don't you?"

I would reply that it was much easier for me to do three inches, then two inches, and then another three inches than it was to attempt to shovel through eight inches of snow at the end of the storm!

This same "shoveling principle" is true in my spiritual life:

- ➢ If I "plow away" the sin before it has a chance to accumulate, the path is clear for God to accomplish His work in me.

- ➢ If I frequently take care of the hidden areas of my heart where sin can pile up—even though it's out of plain sight—my life can shine for Christ in a dark world.

- ➢ If I follow David's example in Psalm 51 and ask God daily to cleanse and purify my heart (whiter than snow!), it makes sense that there won't be an opportunity for the sin to enlarge in its impact and its scope.

Just like plowing away the snow, keeping a short "sin account" keeps the path to victory clear!

—BLH

Today's promise:
God *will* wash your heart whiter than snow!

# DECEMBER 3

Psalm 43:5, NKJV:
"Why are you cast down, O my soul? And why are you disquieted within me? Hope in God; for I shall yet praise Him, The help of my countenance and my God."

---

I confess. I sometimes get discouraged, cast down, and sad in my spirit. That's when my wonderful wife, Brenda, will remind me of this Psalm, and I'll stop to read it or remember it.

With the psalmist, we can all wonder why we are discouraged. It could be due to circumstances, people, or, in reality, anything. But instead of blaming these things, let's obey today's truth-promise: "Hope in God," because He *is* the God of hope (see Romans 15:13).

—JGH

Today's promise:
God *is* the God of hope!

# DECEMBER 4

Psalm 66:3, AMP:
"Say to God, 'How awesome and fearfully glorious are Your works!
Because of the greatness of Your power
Your enemies will pretend to be obedient to You.'"

---

My friend Dorothy and I rented a table and sold some items at a craft sale in Iowa. To entice passersby to stop and look at what we were selling, we set out a basket of candy near the edge of the table. We purchased a pretty large bag of candy to distribute, but before the day was half over, we realized that our candy supply was pretty low, and we still had a half day to go. We set the basket under the table for a while, certain that our beautiful items were the magnet that had drawn in so many shoppers.

That's when we noticed the results that carried a small similarity to those in today's verse: when we had candy, we simply had "intrigued shoppers." When we put the candy away, only the serious lookers—who in most cases purchased something—were the ones who came to our table.

All too often, people who are not truly God's followers try to partake of His power and His glorious works. But God is not fooled by their pretense. We, His children, however, are recipients of His "awesome and fearfully glorious" works. The gratitude this truth-promise ignites in us should also serve as our reminder to share the gospel of Christ to those are intrigued by our God.

—BLH

Today's promise:
God's works *are* "awesome and fearfully glorious!"

# DECEMBER 5

Psalm 104:1, NKJV:
"Bless the Lord, O my soul! O Lord my God,
You are very great: You are clothed with honor and majesty."

God doesn't just do great things. He *is* great! Perhaps that's why the writer of today's truth-promise verse praises God from the depths of his soul.

Additionally, the psalmist sees Him not in human apparel but as having honor and majesty as the clothing that are seen by all who look to Him as their great God.

—BLH

Today's promise:
God *is* great!

# DECEMBER 6

Psalm 34:10, NKJV:
"The young lions lack and suffer hunger;
But those who seek the Lord shall not lack any good thing."

---

We see many different animals in our backyard: deer, squirrels, possums, hawks, rabbits, chipmunks, and all kinds of birds. (Thankfully, there are no lions, as in today's promise verse!)

We particularly enjoy watching the little ones following their mamas, learning the "law of the jungle"—er...yard. Some of the most interesting mamas to watch are the birds: first taking food to their young and then showing them, by example, how to pull the worm from the ground or hover over a flower, waiting for just the right insect to appear. Without their mama's help, the babies would most likely starve.

When the psalmist speaks of the young lions' inability to feed themselves and therefore being hungry, he follows it up with the promise that "those who seek the Lord shall not lack any good thing." I don't know what "any good thing" is. It could be material things that are good for us to have in order to accomplish what God desires of us. It could be spiritual food that feeds our souls.

What I do know is that God's promises are true. If He says we won't lack that good thing, we won't!

—BLH

Today's promise:
You will *not* lack "any good thing."

# DECEMBER 7

Psalm 98:1, NKJV:
"Oh, sing to the Lord a new song!
For He has done marvelous things;
His right hand and His holy arm have gained Him the victory."

---

In Scripture, the mention of God's right hand or of His right arm often refers to His power and authority. The psalmist says in today's truth-promise that God "has done marvelous things." *Webster's New World Dictionary* defines *marvelous* as: "astonishing; extraordinary."

God created the universe in six days and sustains His creation. God sent His Son to die on the cross for our sins. God's Son rose from the dead, defeating death. All of these are marvelous!

This same God loves us. This same God calls us by name, demonstrating that He is interested in us as individuals. This same God provides for us. And this same God is with us.

No wonder He can give us a new song!

—JGH

Today's promise:
God does *marvelous* things!

# DECEMBER 8

Psalm 118:29, NKJV:
"Oh, give thanks to the Lord, for He is good!
For His mercy endures forever."

---

Even though this promise is repeated numerous times throughout this year of devotional thoughts, each time I read it, I seem to see something new. Maybe that's why God included its truths so many times across the pages of Scripture, because it would speak to us in different ways during differing times of need.

The word *endures* struck me with its strength and power today. When my favorite college football team (Go, Irish!) is playing a team of similar caliber, I usually say, "The team with the greater endurance is the team who will win!" And it's usually true. A team who gives up because they're "plum tuckered out" has little endurance. A team who goes so strong at the beginning that they have nothing left to give in the fourth quarter has little endurance. When the team's endurance is lacking, so is its score!

But our amazing God tells us in today's truth-promise that His mercy has staying power. It will be there until the end. It won't give up. It won't quit. It won't leave us without enough strength to accomplish what it was given to us for in the first place. It will endure!

—BLH

Today's promise:
God's mercy *will* endure!

# DECEMBER 9

Isaiah 43:15, KJV:
"I am the Lord, your Holy One, the creator of Israel, your King."

---

I'm always fascinated by the words the Scripture writers choose to describe God. I particularly like when they personalize their descriptions: *my* God; *our* Father; *my* helper.

Perhaps that's why today's truth-promise regarding Who God is caught my eye. God is the One personalizing the relationship in this verse: *your* Holy One; *your* King.

Because of our relationship to Him as His children, we can know Him (through His Word) and interact with Him (in prayer)!

—BLH

Today's promise:
As a believer, you have a *personal* relationship with God!

# DECEMBER 10

Psalm 56:3, KJV:
"Whenever I am afraid, I will trust in You."

---

The fine print. It can include disclaimers, exceptions, and "escape clauses" for the initiator of the document. It makes it so that we are no longer certain of who is trustworthy and who has "fine print" that is there for their good more than for ours.

But in today's truth-promise, the psalmist boldly declares the Lord's unconditional trustworthiness. He uses the word *whenever*, because he knows that no matter what the cause of his fear, He can trust in God.

So can you—*whenever*!

—BLH

Today's promise:
God is *unconditionally* trustworthy!

# DECEMBER 11

Exodus 15:11, ESV:
"Who is like you, O Lord, among the gods?
Who is like you, majestic in holiness,
awesome in glorious deeds, doing wonders?"

---

Moses, in today's truth-promise, asks a question about God: Is there any comparison to God almighty, especially among the idols?

Moses further talks about God's appearance. He says that God's holiness (His absolute moral purity) is incredibly bright, like the sun.

Moses adds that God's *splendor* is fearfully wondrous and majestic (*Webster's New World Dictionary*).

Not only are God's appearance and person incredible, but His actions are supernatural. Think of the wonders God did in Egypt with Pharaoh, with the Egyptian plagues, and with the parting of the Red Sea (to name a few).

We can answer Moses's question: *No one* compares to our great God!

—JGH

Today's promise:
Your great God *will* do wonders!

# DECEMBER 12

Psalm 54:4, ESV:
"Behold, God is my helper;
the Lord is the upholder of my life."

———

When I am weary, He holds me up.

When I feel as if I can run the race of life no longer, He holds me up.

When my gaze drops downward toward the valley into which I am falling, He holds me up.

When I am crumpling onto the ground because of the words and actions that have been thrown at me and around me, He holds me up.

When the trial seems too much to bear, He holds me up.

When I start to collapse because I am spiritually hungry and thirsty, He holds me up.

Friend, His strong arms are there to help you. He will hold you up.

—BLH

Today's promise:
God *will* uphold you!

# DECEMBER 13

Matthew 5:8, 11–12, NKJV:
"Blessed are the pure in heart, for they shall see God. Blessed are you when they revile and persecute you, and say all kinds of evil against you falsely for My sake. Rejoice and be exceedingly glad, for great is your reward in heaven, for so they persecuted the prophets who were before you."

---

We read in church history with reverence and wonder the stories of the martyrs of the faith. In our land of religious freedom, we can't fully conceive of religious persecution happening. However, persecution for the gospel of Christ is present in the world. It costs some of our brothers and sisters in Christ their lives—simply for being believers and doing right for God.

Persecution for Christ can take many forms. It might be physical, but it can also be verbal. It can be in the marketplace or in the schoolroom. It can even come from "religious" sources.

While we should be gracious in our Christian testimony, God promises that we can endure persecution for Christ in whatever form it comes, and we can do so with joy instead of with fear.

"Yet if anyone suffers as a Christian, let him not be ashamed, but let him glorify God in this matter" (1 Peter 4:16, NKJV).

—JGH

Today's promise:
God *will* reward those who are persecuted for His sake.

# DECEMBER 14

2 Corinthians 9:8, NASB:
"And God is able to make all grace abound to you, so that always having all sufficiency in everything, you may have an abundance for every good deed."

---

My "ideal Saturday" turned into a reality: favorite magazine arrived in the mail; lifetime friend sent me a box of fall-fragrance candles; rain fell gently, creating an overcast softness outside; and God let me know that He was more than enough.

It's that last thought that I want you to remember today.

Whatever your circumstances...

Whatever your marital status...

Whatever your longings...

Whatever your physical needs...

Whatever your spiritual needs...

Whatever your emotional needs...

Whatever your financial needs...

Whatever it is that leaves you feeling incomplete...

Whatever your future holds...

"God is able to make all grace abound to you."

—BLH

Today's promise:
God *is* more than enough!

# DECEMBER 15

Psalm 40:17, ESV:
"As for me, I am poor and needy, but the Lord takes thought
for me. You are my help and my deliverer;
do not delay, O my God!"

---

The psalmist knew that he had nothing to offer to God in exchange for His help. Today's truth-promise also tells us that the writer knew that in spite of his inability to earn God's care, God was already thinking about him, helping him, and delivering him.

Perhaps that's why he simply stated, "Do not delay," knowing that God was aware and was already there to help.

—BLH

Today's promise:
God *is already there*!

# DECEMBER 16

Revelation 1:8, AMP:
"'I am the Alpha and the Omega [the Beginning and the End],' says the Lord God, 'Who is [existing forever] and Who was [continually existing in the past] and Who is to come, the Almighty [the Omnipotent, the Ruler of all].'"

---

How do you grasp the concept and truth of God almighty, the One Who is "the Beginning and the End" of all? The answer is: you can't.

How do you understand God almighty, the One Who was in eternity, Who is now in time, and Who "is to come"? The answer is: you can't.

How do you comprehend God almighty, the One Who is all in all and Who is omnipresent, omnipotent, and omniscient? Again, the answer is: you can't.

A God you could grasp, understand, and comprehend would not be almighty God. You simply believe Him, accept Him, receive Him, and live for Him!

—JGH

Today's promise:
Your *almighty God* exists forever!

# DECEMBER 17

Philippians 4:13, AMP:
"I can do all things [which He has called me to do] through Him who strengthens and empowers me [to fulfill His purpose—I am self-sufficient in Christ's sufficiency; I am ready for anything and equal to anything through Him who infuses me with inner strength and confident peace.]"

---

The trouble with an oft-quoted verse like today's truth-promise is that we tend to dim the intensity of the depth of its meaning as we soon find ourselves flippantly quoting it. We whip it out like an adhesive bandage to apply to our spiritual "owies," forgetting the power of its truths.

Yet this verse is the empowering agent God often uses to remind us:

It is He Who strengthens us "to fulfill His purpose."

It is He Who enables us to do what "He has called [us] to do."

It is He Who "infuses [us] with inner strength."

It is He Who gives us "confident peace."

"*It is He.*" Not us, but Christ. (See Galatians 2:20.)

—BLH

Today's promise:
You *can* do all things through Christ!

# DECEMBER 18

Isaiah 48:17, ESV:
"Thus says the Lord, your Redeemer, the Holy One of Israel:
'I am the Lord your God, who teaches you to profit,
who leads you in the way you should go.'"

---

God, the Redeemer, the Holy One of Israel, the Lord our God—our Teacher and Leader! He takes the time to personally teach us His benefits ("profit"). And while we're on that word, *benefits*, Psalm 68:19 (KJV) states that God "daily loadeth us with benefits." (Wow!)

But today's truth-promise takes it even further: God then leads us in the way that we should go! His truth guides us, prepares us, and shows us the next step to take on our spiritual journey.

—BLH

Today's promise:
God *will* teach you and lead you!

# DECEMBER 19

Psalm 77:1, AMP:
"My voice rises to God, and I will cry aloud;
My voice rises to God, and He will hear me."

———

The God we love, worship, and serve is a prayer-hearing, prayer-answering God. God, the creator and sustainer of the universe, actually listens to our prayers!

There is no language barrier, no physical barrier, and no time barrier that can keep Him from hearing.

He hears our prayer for salvation.

He hears our prayers for help and guidance.

He hears our prayers for others.

No idol hears prayers. No inanimate object hears prayers. Only God can hear our prayers!

—JGH

Today's promise:
God *will* hear your prayer!

# DECEMBER 20

Psalm 78:38, AMP:
"But He, the source of compassion and lovingkindness,
forgave their wickedness and did not destroy them;
Many times He restrained His anger
And did not stir up all His wrath."

---

Our God is not mean; He is repeatedly merciful. He gives us what we *don't* deserve and keeps from us what we *do* deserve.

Our God is also holy and just and cannot ignore sin. However, God's abundant compassion found a way for Him to judge sin and yet allow the *forgiveness* of sin to us (sinners). His way was accomplished through our Savior's death on the cross.

All praise and glory to God for His merciful forgiveness and lovingkindness.

—JGH

Today's promise:
Your compassionate God *will* forgive your sin.

# DECEMBER 21

Psalm 34:4, AMP:
"I sought the Lord [on the authority of His word], and He answered me, and delivered me from all my fears."

---

We had a relatively small wedding ceremony, and throughout the ceremony our pastor intertwined fun and interesting elements about our unique relationship with the teachings about marriage that are found in God's Word. The gathering and celebration that day was just as we had hoped it would be. But we'll let you in on a little "funny" from our wedding.

We drove out of the church parking lot after waving one final farewell to our guests and came to the stop sign down the road from the church. That was when we looked at each other and realized that we had never signed the marriage license! We quickly grabbed the phone to call the pastor (to make sure he didn't leave before we got back), and he met us in the parking lot with the marriage license, which had been in his jacket pocket since before the wedding ceremony—for safe keeping! We signed it and went on our merry (or "marry," if you will) way! That single piece of paper held the earthly legal authority to prove that we were married that day.

Today's truth-promise from God authoritative Word tells us that because of what He has recorded for us to know about Him, we can be assured that when we seek Him, He will answer us. In so doing, we will find ourselves delivered from our fears!

—BLH

Today's promise:
God's authoritative Word *assures* you of His promises!

# DECEMBER 22

Exodus 34:5–6, ESV:
"The Lord descended in the cloud and stood with him there, and proclaimed the name of the Lord. The Lord passed before him and proclaimed, 'The Lord, the Lord, a God merciful and gracious, slow to anger, and abounding in steadfast love and faithfulness.'"

---

The Lord Himself is the One Who declared today's truth-promise. He was speaking to Moses, His friend (see Exodus 33:11), and identifying Himself by both His name and His attributes.

If you've ever read or heard anything about the fluctuating devotion of the children of Israel (both to Moses and to God), you will see quite easily how they would know firsthand that God was:

- ✓ merciful,
- ✓ gracious,
- ✓ slow to anger,
- ✓ abounding in steadfast love, and
- ✓ abounding in faithfulness.

And because He chose to record this conversation in His timeless and eternal Word, we know that He possesses those same attributes in His dealings with us today!

—BLH

Today's promise:
God *is* slow to anger!

# DECEMBER 23

Luke 1:32, KJV:
"He shall be great, and shall be called the Son of the Highest: and the Lord God shall give unto him the throne of his father David."

---

God's Son.

Great in all things and in all ways. Son of the Highest. Future King of kings.

What a promise divine!

—BLH

Today's promise:
Christ *will* be the King of kings!

# DECEMBER 24

Isaiah 7:14, KJV:
"Therefore the Lord himself shall give you a sign; Behold, a virgin shall conceive, and bear a son, and shall call his name Immanuel."

---

Hundreds of years before Jesus Christ was born, his birth was promised through the prophet Isaiah. That in itself is amazing.

But God's attention to detail in His promises is no coincidence! He said that the virgin would conceive a Child, that the Child would be a boy, and that His name would be Immanuel, meaning, "God with us."

Luke 2 tells how this prophecy was fulfilled: a young virgin, Mary, conceived a child, though she had never had intimate relations with a man. When the time came for her to have the child, He was a boy. He was named Jesus, which signified that He (God among us) would save us from our sins.

Wow! Wonderful fulfillment of prophecy. More than wonderful promise!

—BLH

Today's promise:
God is *with* you!

# DECEMBER 25

Matthew 1:21, KJV:
"And she shall bring forth a son, and thou shalt call his name Jesus: for he shall save his people from their sins."

———

What better promise today than one that reminds us why God's Son—this loving, precious Jesus—came to earth.

This loving, precious Jesus came to bring hope to the hopeless.

This loving, precious Jesus came to bring light to the darkness.

This loving, precious Jesus came to bring joy to the sorrowful.

This loving, precious Jesus left His Father's perfect, holy, glorious home in heaven to fulfill a promise: to save His people from their sins.

Gift of all gifts!

Joy of all joys!

Promise of all promises!

—BLH

Today's promise:
He *will* save those who call on His name!

# DECEMBER 26

Luke 2:10–14, KJV:
"And the angel said unto them, 'Fear not: for, behold, I bring you good tidings of great joy, which shall be to all people. For unto you is born this day in the city of David a Saviour, which is Christ the Lord. And this shall be a sign unto you; Ye shall find the babe wrapped in swaddling clothes, lying in a manger.'
And suddenly there was with the angel a multitude of the heavenly host praising God, and saying, 'Glory to God in the highest, and on earth peace, good will toward men.'"

---

While we hope you had a blessed Christmas, we want to remind you that the Christmas celebration isn't over. Sorry, we can't promise you more gifts or yummy treats!

However, we *can* share with you the promise from these verses: the good news of our Savior's birth—the "gospel"—is for all people! And we are to share it with everyone!

"And He said to them, 'Go into all the world and preach the gospel to all creation'" (Mark 16:15, NASB).

—BLH

Today's promise:
God's good news *will* bring great joy!

# DECEMBER 27

Isaiah 50:7, NKJV:
"For the Lord God will help Me;
therefore I will not be disgraced; therefore I have set My face
like a flint, and I know that I will not be ashamed."

---

Our God is not a God of confusion. His help, then, is clear—not contradictory or confusing. His help is sure and sufficient.

Therefore, we can boldly confront whatever is facing us—without fear or concern for disgrace or shame (which might come if we were to act without His help).

—JGH

Today's promise:
God *will* help you!

# DECEMBER 28

Deuteronomy 20:4, ESV:
"For the Lord your God is he who goes with you to fight for you against your enemies, to give you the victory."

———

God will go *with* you...

to fight *for* you...

and to give *you* the victory!

—BLH

Today's promise:
God *will* give you the victory!

# DECEMBER 29

1 Kings 2:3, NKJV:
"And keep the charge of the Lord your God: to walk in His ways, to keep His statutes, His commandments, His judgments, and His testimonies, as it is written in the Law of Moses, that you may prosper in all that you do and wherever you turn."

---

King David's life was coming to an end, and he was sharing some final wisdom with his son Solomon in this verse. It was taken in part from some of the words that Moses had shared with his successor, Joshua (see Deuteronomy 31:6), and that God had later reiterated to Joshua (see Joshua 1:7, 9) and then included in His eternal Word to share with us!

The prosperity of God's abundant blessing is promised to those who fulfill their obligation (AMP) to keep God's charge:

- to walk in His ways;
- to keep His statutes;
- to keep His commandments;
- to keep His judgments; and
- to keep His testimonies.

—BLH

Today's promise:
God *will* bless you when you follow His teaching!

# DECEMBER 30

Joshua 21:45, ESV:
"Not one word of all the good promises that the Lord had made to the house of Israel had failed; all came to pass."

---

My recent readings have been from Joshua and Judges, and I have been struck anew with the whining and grumbling of God's people. These people had *gazillions* of amazing things happen right in front of their very eyes: two times God parted massive amounts of water and held it in place while they walked across on dry land! Weaponless, they conquered a city secured by a seemingly insurmountable wall, and from a human point of view, they did it with nothing but their voices and some trumpets! Over and over again their needs (and wants) were met. Their response? They gave Him short-lived gratitude and worship followed by a long-term pattern of selfishness and complaining.

Over and over again my needs (and often wants) are met. I have the completed Word of God from which to read and learn. I have salvation from what I deserve. I have life. And yet I complain. And in so doing, I literally question His promises and His love.

However, His love and mercy never fail! In fact, He *promise*d that they wouldn't! He keeps His promises—in His time, in His way, and for His glory!

Because of His great mercy, grace, and unfailing love, and because the God of Joshua is our God too, we can take an Old Testament truth about God and apply it in a personal way:

"Not one word of all the good promises that the Lord had made to \_\_\_\_\_(your name here)\_\_\_\_\_ had failed; all came to pass!"

—BLH

Today's promise:
God *will* keep His promises!

# DECEMBER 31

Psalm 65:11, NKJV:
"You crown the year with Your goodness,
And Your paths drip with abundance."

---

It's been a year filled with promises taken straight from the Word of God. Thank you for joining us on this journey. Regardless of the events of the past year, we can all join the psalmist in one final truth-promise that compels us to praise God.

It was our desire that as you were spiritually, emotionally, and even physically refreshed, you would come to see that the promises of God were carried out in a way that is always and only good.

Though not *everything* that happened throughout your year *seemed* good, God, in His infinite wisdom, knew what was best for you. He not only withheld from you what you deserved (eternal punishment for your sin) but also gave you what you did not deserve (His unfailing grace).

One of our primary motivations this year was to help you look through the lens of His promises and see that He was there—every month, every day, every moment—dripping an abundance of His mercy every step of the way!

May the year ahead continue to be one in which we are learning from, leaning on, and more fully loving our great promise-keeping God!

—BLH/JGH

Today's promise:
God *will* crown your year with His goodness!

# SCRIPTURE INDEX

Genesis 16:13 ................................. 165
Genesis 28:15 ................................. 136
Genesis 41:51 ................................. 247
Genesis 50:20 ................................. 247
Exodus 14 ....................................... 46
Exodus 14:13–14 ........................... 163
Exodus 15:2 .................................... 211
Exodus 15:11 .................................. 353
Exodus 20:12 ........................ 249, 253
Exodus 33:11 .................................. 364
Exodus 34:5–6 ................................ 364
Numbers 23:19 .............................. 156
Deuteronomy 4:23–24 .................. 153
Deuteronomy 4:29 .......................... 40
Deuteronomy 7:9 ........................... 240
Deuteronomy 20:4 ......................... 370
Deuteronomy 31:6 ...... 9, 13, 136, 371
Deuteronomy 31:8 ......................... 272
Deuteronomy 32:4 ............. 112, 338
Deuteronomy 33:27 ......................... 12
Joshua 1:7, 9 ................................... 371
Joshua 1:9 ....................................... 204
Joshua 21:45 ................................... 372
1 Samuel 15:22 ............................... 152
2 Samuel 7:28 ................................. 189
2 Samuel 22:31 ................................. 36
1 Kings 2:3 ...................................... 371
1 Chronicles 28:9 .......................... 288
2 Chronicles 16:9 ........................... 167
2 Chronicles 20:6 .......................... 325
Nehemiah 8:10 ....................... 66, 142
Job 5:7 ............................................. 260
Job 5:17 ............................................. 67
Job 23:10 ........................................... 39
Job 42:2 ........................................... 137
Psalm 1:1–2 .................................... 199
Psalm 1:6 .......................................... 84
Psalm 3:5 .......................................... 92
Psalm 5:11 ....................................... 214
Psalm 5:12 ....................................... 177
Psalm 7:11 ........................................ 111
Psalm 9:9–10 .................................... 51
Psalm 11:7 ........................................ 111
Psalm 16:8 ...................................... 182
Psalm 16:11 ...................................... 29
Psalm 18:30 ...................................... 84
Psalm 18:31–32 .............................. 281
Psalm 23 ......................................... 202

Psalm 23:1 ...................................... 283
Psalm 23:4 ...................................... 183
Psalm 25:4–5 .................................... 75
Psalm 25:9 ...................................... 141
Psalm 27:1 ...................................... 228
Psalm 27:5 ........................................ 31
Psalm 27:13 .................................... 287
Psalm 27:14 .................... 19, 287, 340
Psalm 28:7 ...................................... 203
Psalm 29:11 .................................... 302
Psalm 30:2 ...................................... 196
Psalm 31:7 ...................................... 236
Psalm 31:19 .................................... 231
Psalm 31:22 .................................... 303
Psalm 31:23–24 .............................. 183
Psalm 32:1 ...................................... 148
Psalm 32:8 ...................................... 298
Psalm 33:10–11 .............................. 118
Psalm 34:4 ...................................... 363
Psalm 34:8 ...................................... 120
Psalm 34:9 ...................................... 283
Psalm 34:10 .................................... 348
Psalm 34:15 ...................................... 60
Psalm 34:17 ...................................... 85
Psalm 36:8 ...................................... 322
Psalm 37:11 .................................... 144
Psalm 37:23 ...................................... 21
Psalm 37:39 .................................... 107
Psalm 38:15 .................................... 139
Psalm 40:17 .................................... 357
Psalm 43:5 ...................................... 345
Psalm 44:4 ...................................... 280
Psalm 46:1 ...................................... 187
Psalm 46:10 ...................................... 35
Psalm 48:10 .................................... 126
Psalm 48:14 .................................... 250
Psalm 50:15 .................................... 215
Psalm 51:6 ...................................... 341
Psalm 51:7 ...................................... 344
Psalm 51:10 .............................. 23, 201
Psalm 51:12 .................................... 300
Psalm 51:17 .................................... 152
Psalm 54:4 ...................................... 354
Psalm 55:17 ...................................... 44
Psalm 55:22 ...................................... 30
Psalm 56:3 ...................................... 352
Psalm 56:9 ...................................... 138
Psalm 57:3 ........................................ 63

| | |
|---|---|
| Psalm 57:10 | 50 |
| Psalm 59:17 | 239 |
| Psalm 60:11–12 | 198 |
| Psalm 61:3 | 180 |
| Psalm 62:2 | 89 |
| Psalm 62:5 | 174, 289 |
| Psalm 62:7 | 86 |
| Psalm 62:8 | 327 |
| Psalm 63:3 | 143 |
| Psalm 65:11 | 373 |
| Psalm 66:3 | 346 |
| Psalm 68:19 | 360 |
| Psalm 70:5 | 209 |
| Psalm 71:20 | 47 |
| Psalm 73:24 | 305 |
| Psalm 73:26 | 101 |
| Psalm 77:1 | 361 |
| Psalm 78:34 | 104 |
| Psalm 78:35 | 104 |
| Psalm 78:38 | 362 |
| Psalm 81:10 | 317 |
| Psalm 84:12 | 293 |
| Psalm 86:5 | 246 |
| Psalm 86:7 | 320 |
| Psalm 89:33 | 158 |
| Psalm 91:1 | 34 |
| Psalm 91:2 | 113 |
| Psalm 91:14 | 160 |
| Psalm 91:15 | 178 |
| Psalm 92:5 | 312 |
| Psalm 92:12–15 | 335 |
| Psalm 97:1 | 292 |
| Psalm 97:7 | 292 |
| Psalm 98:1 | 349 |
| Psalm 99:5 | 126 |
| Psalm 100:5 | 61, 133 |
| Psalm 102:27 | 315 |
| Psalm 103:8 | 244 |
| Psalm 103:11 | 223 |
| Psalm 103:12 | 155, 164 |
| Psalm 104:1 | 347 |
| Psalm 106:1 | 282 |
| Psalm 107:1 | 135 |
| Psalm 107:8 | 213 |
| Psalm 108:12–13 | 260 |
| Psalm 112:4 | 70 |
| Psalm 115:13 | 218 |
| Psalm 116:6–8 | 263 |
| Psalm 116:15 | 96 |
| Psalm 117:2 | 61 |
| Psalm 118:1 | 243 |
| Psalm 118:6 | 170 |
| Psalm 118:14 | 142 |
| Psalm 118:23 | 254 |
| Psalm 118:29 | 350 |
| Psalm 119:2 | 81 |
| Psalm 119:32 | 238 |
| Psalm 119:49–50 | 191 |
| Psalm 119:68 | 195 |
| Psalm 119:105 | 29 |
| Psalm 119:130 | 228 |
| Psalm 119:137 | 117 |
| Psalm 119:160 | 87 |
| Psalm 119:172 | 147 |
| Psalm 120:1 | 69 |
| Psalm 121:2 | 248 |
| Psalm 121:3 | 123 |
| Psalm 121:5 | 323 |
| Psalm 125:2 | 173 |
| Psalm 126:6 | 80 |
| Psalm 128:1–4 | 234 |
| Psalm 138:7 | 46 |
| Psalm 139:2–4 | 188 |
| Psalm 139:7–10 | 207 |
| Psalm 139:15–18 | 16 |
| Psalm 139:23–24 | 188 |
| Psalm 144:15 | 197 |
| Psalm 145:8 | 311 |
| Psalm 145:9 | 38 |
| Psalm 145:14 | 194 |
| Psalm 145:17 | 95 |
| Psalm 145:20 | 279 |
| Psalm 147:3 | 247 |
| Psalm 147:4 | 224 |
| Psalm 147:5 | 79, 121 |
| Psalm 147:11 | 268 |
| Proverbs 2:6 | 216 |
| Proverbs 2:7 | 241 |
| Proverbs 3:6 | 125 |
| Proverbs 3:12 | 134 |
| Proverbs 3:13, 15–17 | 291 |
| Proverbs 3:18 | 82 |
| Proverbs 4:10 | 253 |
| Proverbs 8:17 | 232 |
| Proverbs 8:32–33 | 227 |
| Proverbs 10:4 | 64 |
| Proverbs 12:25 | 191 |
| Proverbs 14:26 | 319 |
| Proverbs 15:3 | 124 |
| Proverbs 16:3 | 20, 49 |
| Proverbs 19:21 | 330 |
| Proverbs 25:20 | 93 |
| Proverbs 30:17 | 249 |
| Isaiah 7:14 | 366 |

| Reference | Page |
|---|---|
| Isaiah 12:2 | 100, 286 |
| Isaiah 12:3 | 258, 306, 322 |
| Isaiah 26:3 | 132 |
| Isaiah 26:4 | 157 |
| Isaiah 30:1 | 329 |
| Isaiah 30:15 | 329 |
| Isaiah 30:18 | 169 |
| Isaiah 30:21 | 141 |
| Isaiah 40:8 | 205 |
| Isaiah 40:28 | 121 |
| Isaiah 40:31 | 54, 55, 56, 57, 58 |
| Isaiah 41:10 | 43 |
| Isaiah 41:13 | 17, 215 |
| Isaiah 42:8 | 274 |
| Isaiah 43:1 | 235 |
| Isaiah 43:2 | 41, 46 |
| Isaiah 43:10–11 | 150 |
| Isaiah 43:15 | 351 |
| Isaiah 43:25 | 155 |
| Isaiah 46:4 | 179 |
| Isaiah 48:17 | 360 |
| Isaiah 50:4 | 93 |
| Isaiah 50:7 | 369 |
| Isaiah 52:12 | 173 |
| Isaiah 53:6 | 270 |
| Isaiah 54:10 | 245 |
| Isaiah 55:9 | 328 |
| Isaiah 55:11 | 24, 205 |
| Isaiah 57:17 | 315 |
| Isaiah 61:3 | 254 |
| Isaiah 64:4 | 294 |
| Isaiah 65:24 | 130 |
| Jeremiah 9:23–24 | 309 |
| Jeremiah 10:2–5 | 334 |
| Jeremiah 10:6 | 334 |
| Jeremiah 10:10 | 331 |
| Jeremiah 10:13 | 340 |
| Jeremiah 14:22 | 289 |
| Jeremiah 17:7–8 | 332 |
| Jeremiah 17:14 | 48 |
| Jeremiah 18:4 | 264 |
| Jeremiah 23:23–24 | 165 |
| Jeremiah 27:5 | 337 |
| Jeremiah 31:3 | 53 |
| Jeremiah 32:17 | 28, 313 |
| Jeremiah 32:27 | 313 |
| Jeremiah 33:3 | 119 |
| Lamentations 3:22–23 | 59 |
| Lamentations 3:23 | 221 |
| Lamentations 3:24 | 295 |
| Lamentations 3:25 | 340 |
| Daniel 2:20–21 | 296 |
| Micah 7:18 | 155 |
| Nahum 1:7 | 73 |
| Matthew 1:21 | 367 |
| Matthew 5:3 | 23 |
| Matthew 5:5 | 144 |
| Matthew 5:6 | 322 |
| Matthew 5:7 | 297 |
| Matthew 5:8 | 27 |
| Matthew 5:8, 11–12 | 355 |
| Matthew 5:9 | 237 |
| Matthew 6:8 | 130 |
| Matthew 6:33 | 11 |
| Matthew 7:7 | 208 |
| Matthew 7:11 | 317 |
| Matthew 7:24–25 | 271 |
| Matthew 10:29–31 | 326 |
| Matthew 11:28 | 110 |
| Matthew 11:29 | 267 |
| Matthew 19:26 | 275 |
| Matthew 28:18–20 | 78 |
| Mark 10:17 | 103 |
| Mark 10:18 | 103 |
| Mark 10:26–27 | 290 |
| Mark 16:15 | 368 |
| Luke 1:32 | 365 |
| Luke 2 | 366 |
| Luke 2:10–14 | 368 |
| Luke 5:12 | 265 |
| Luke 6:22 | 200 |
| Luke 6:38 | 192 |
| Luke 8:5–15 | 80 |
| Luke 11:13 | 284 |
| Luke 11:28 | 321 |
| Luke 15:11-12 | 295 |
| Luke 16:17 | 33 |
| John 1:16 | 83 |
| John 3:16 | 42 |
| John 4:14 | 306 |
| John 6:47 | 115 |
| John 8:12 | 128 |
| John 8:36 | 217 |
| John 9:1–3 | 255 |
| John 10:2–3 | 235 |
| John 10:9–10 | 68 |
| John 10:10 | 339 |
| John 10:28 | 77 |
| John 10:30 | 103 |
| John 13:15, 17 | 52 |
| John 13:35 | 242 |
| John 14:2–3 | 122 |
| John 14:3 | 18 |
| John 14:9 | 103 |

| | |
|---|---|
| John 14:16–17 | 269 |
| John 15:5 | 226 |
| John 15:12 | 266 |
| John 15:15 | 336 |
| John 16:13 | 127 |
| John 16:33 | 161 |
| John 17:17 | 299 |
| John 19:30 | 259 |
| John 20:29 | 229 |
| Acts 1:8 | 98 |
| Acts 2:21 | 108 |
| Acts 4:12 | 131 |
| Acts 10:34 | 268 |
| Acts 17:6 | 98 |
| Acts 17:24–25 | 307 |
| Acts 20:32 | 172 |
| Acts 26:8 | 176 |
| Romans 2:11 | 268, 338 |
| Romans 3:23 | 112 |
| Romans 5:8 | 256 |
| Romans 5:9 | 184 |
| Romans 6:14 | 333 |
| Romans 8:1 | 62 |
| Romans 8:15–17 | 222 |
| Romans 8:26 | 15 |
| Romans 8:28 | 62 |
| Romans 8:29 | 45 |
| Romans 8:31 | 62 |
| Romans 8:35–37 | 220 |
| Romans 8:38–39 | 62, 245, 277 |
| Romans 10:13 | 206 |
| Romans 10:17 | 225 |
| Romans 11:33 | 162 |
| Romans 12:2 | 137 |
| Romans 12:21 | 193 |
| Romans 15:4 | 191, 230 |
| Romans 15:5 | 175 |
| Romans 15:13 | 29, 345 |
| 1 Corinthians 1:9 | 106 |
| 1 Corinthians 6:19–20 | 219 |
| 1 Corinthians 8:6 | 171 |
| 1 Corinthians 10:13 | 221, 279 |
| 1 Corinthians 13:4–8 | 193 |
| 1 Corinthians 15:58 | 90 |
| 2 Corinthians 1:3–4 | 97 |
| 2 Corinthians 1:20 | 70, 76 |
| 2 Corinthians 12:9 | 257 |
| 2 Corinthians 13:11 | 116 |
| Galatians 2:20 | 359 |
| Galatians 3:13 | 300 |
| Galatians 6:9 | 114 |
| Ephesians 1:7 | 235 |
| Ephesians 1:7–8 | 301 |
| Ephesians 2:4–5 | 276 |
| Ephesians 2:8 | 154, 251 |
| Ephesians 2:10 | 212 |
| Ephesians 3:20 | 15, 37, 317 |
| Ephesians 6:2 | 249 |
| Ephesians 6:2–3 | 25, 253 |
| Ephesians 6:16 | 26 |
| Philippians 1:6 | 45 |
| Philippians 2:5 | 328 |
| Philippians 2:13 | 151 |
| Philippians 4:5 | 186 |
| Philippians 4:6 | 141 |
| Philippians 4:6–7 | 159 |
| Philippians 4:8 | 141 |
| Philippians 4:9 | 141 |
| Philippians 4:13 | 113, 359 |
| Philippians 4:19 | 14 |
| Colossians 1:13–14 | 261 |
| Colossians 2:10 | 259 |
| Colossians 3:1 | 29, 316 |
| 1 Thessalonians 2:13 | 278 |
| 1 Thessalonians 5:13–14 | 237 |
| 1 Thessalonians 5:24 | 32 |
| 1 Timothy 1:17 | 94 |
| 1 Timothy 2:5–6 | 308 |
| 1 Timothy 6:6 | 23 |
| 1 Timothy 6:17 | 168 |
| 2 Timothy 1:7 | 181 |
| 2 Timothy 3:7 | 216 |
| 2 Timothy 3:16 | 129 |
| Titus 1:2 | 9 |
| Titus 3:5 | 290 |
| Titus 3:5–6 | 210 |
| Hebrews 4:12 | 342 |
| Hebrews 4:16 | 318 |
| Hebrews 6:10 | 145 |
| Hebrews 8:12 | 155 |
| Hebrews 10:23 | 76 |
| Hebrews 12:1–3 | 57 |
| Hebrews 12:2 | 154, 200, 283 |
| Hebrews 12:28–29 | 153 |
| Hebrews 13:5 | 99, 136 |
| Hebrews 13:6 | 262 |
| Hebrews 13:20–21 | 343 |
| James 1:5 | 10 |
| James 1:13 | 140 |
| James 1:17 | 88 |
| James 1:25 | 22 |
| James 3:6 | 63 |
| James 4:3 | 208 |
| James 4:6 | 74, 280 |

| | |
|---|---|
| James 4:7 | 314 |
| James 4:8 | 109 |
| James 4:10 | 146 |
| 1 Peter 1:8 | 229 |
| 1 Peter 1:23–25 | 102 |
| 1 Peter 3:14–15 | 185 |
| 1 Peter 4:16 | 355 |
| 2 Peter 1:3 | 81, 321 |
| 2 Peter 1:3–4 | 175, 252 |
| 2 Peter 3:9 | 190, 225 |
| 1 John 1:9 | 233, 304 |
| 1 John 2:1–2 | 304 |
| 1 John 2:15–17 | 285 |
| 1 John 2:25 | 65, 71 |
| 1 John 2:26 | 71 |
| 1 John 3:1 | 235 |
| 1 John 3:19–20 | 91 |
| 1 John 4:4 | 161 |
| 1 John 4:7–8 | 242 |
| 1 John 4:18 | 228 |
| 1 John 4:18–19 | 324 |
| 1 John 5:19–20 | 273 |
| Jude 24 | 45 |
| Revelation 1:3 | 342 |
| Revelation 1:8 | 358 |
| Revelation 1:19 | 310 |
| Revelation 21:1 | 155 |
| Revelation 21:4 | 310 |
| Revelation 21:5 | 155 |
| Revelation 21:6 | 100 |

# ABOUT THE AUTHORS

**Brenda (Strohbehn) Henderson** launched her faith-based blog, *Petals from the Basket* (PetalsfromtheBasket.com), in March 2012. As a woman who married for the first time at the age of fifty-five, Brenda brings a unique insight to the needs, joys, and concerns of women of all ages and from every marital status.

**Joe Henderson**, a retired international airline pilot, is lovingly called "Captain Joe" by all who know him well. Joe has joined Brenda in her love for writing and frequently contributes to her blog via "The Captain's Corner," where he intertwines his familiarity with the airline industry with practical biblical lessons.

The Hendersons reside in Indiana, where they are active in their local church and enjoy writing, fishing in neighboring ponds, spending time with family, entertaining, and cheering on the Notre Dame football team!

# THE HENDERSONS' BOOKS

**By Joe Henderson:**

*The Captain's Corner: A 21-Day Devotional*
*The Praise Project: Intentional Praise for 31 Days*

**By Brenda Henderson:**

*Choosing to Change when Change Happens*
*Petals from the Basket*
*Petals from the Basket (Book 2)*
*Petals from the Basket (Book 3)*
*Petals of Gratitude*
*The A-Z Guide to Promoting Your Self-Published Book*

**By Joe and Brenda Henderson:**

*Pages of Promises: 365 Devotional Thoughts on the Promises of God*

All of the Hendersons' books are available through Amazon and Barnes and Noble.

Made in the USA
Columbia, SC
05 December 2024